FACING THE HUNTER

DAVID ADAMS RICHARDS

FACING THE HUNTER

Reflections on a Misunderstood Pursuit

DOUBLEDAY CANADA

Doubleday Canada and colophon are registered trademarks

Library and Archives Canada Cataloguing in Publication

Richards, David Adams, 1950-
Facing the hunter / David Adams Richards.

ISBN 978-0-385-25918-7

1. Hunting—Canada. 2. Richards, David Adams, 1950-.
I. Title.

SK151.R53 2011   799.2971   C2011-900124-1

Printed and bound in the USA

Published in Canada by Doubleday Canada,
a division of Random House of Canada Limited

Visit Random House of Canada Limited's website: www.randomhouse.ca

10 9 8 7 6 5 4 3 2 1

For Giles Kenny, Gary Wood, Ed McIntyre

Prologue

"Progressive" is such a damnable word. In the middle-class lexicon "progressive" now means that most of the people I have known and loved are somehow less than others, who think and rationalize about compassion and fairness.

As a case in point, I grew up with boys from rural New Brunswick who would bring their guns to school, so they could hunt on the way back home. I know we cannot do this today—I am not saying we should. But rifles were not something naturally feared when I was a boy. They became a part of a society feared by whole sections of intellectuals, who tell us that it is only conservatives and right-wingers who are paranoid about the "other." Most of the people determined to align rifles with murder and thugs have never handled rifles—and don't know the differences between them. In our modern novels, most often the hunter is also the subhuman, not a man of any grace or courage—unless the hunter is a First Nations man. They cannot be seen to be the "other." Of course I am not saying they should ever be—but in a strange paradox, First Nations people are actually recognized as "other" by many academics now, because of a kind of moral favouritism.

But there is little favouritism shown to those who wish to stop the gun registry. Those who want that are, well, conservative, and less compassionate. And they do not think like us, the fair-minded ones.

A few years back I was in a house in Edmonton, Alberta, overhearing how deplorable it was for men to work in the oil patch, to hunt with weapons, to kill the ecology we all must share. It was as if I was listening to a lecture directed at me by a neophyte poet across the room. The poet who was deploring all of this was warmed by oil and well fed by buffet and had a captive audience everywhere about him that night, as he sipped a Chardonnay. Of course I suspect in his whole life he had never gotten truly drunk, or at least never gone on one. And he lived in a society every bit as closeted and insulated as did those tenured clerics in the time of Old John of Gaunt. Perhaps he never considered this.

I suppose I have always disliked men like this, clever enough to have expensive cloth covering their arses, and pleased to carry with them a register of human complaint and a suspicion of certain jobs and of so, so many people. Their ideals are those of a subversion to a tradition that, so often, they have never themselves encountered. They are the transgressionalists who have chosen their targets very carefully, so as never to be alone. It is a very strange way to show liberal empathy. Which, of course, is what they promote among themselves. Or at least what that poet promoted that evening.

Still, my ideas wouldn't be readily accepted that night.

If rifles fit in with his admonishing, so hunting must as well. And it is not in any way my policy to convince anyone that hunting is noble, or that hunting cannot be wilfully cruel. My only suggestion to the world is that those who eat meat should be morally obligated to kill at least once in their lives that which they eat. After two months without oil, as ill conceived as the oil patch is and as ill fated as our time-honoured traditions seem to be, that generous poet would no longer be sipping his wine at the buffet deploring those without his intellectual and sarcastic capacity. And those women who surrounded him, nodding their heads at those terrible people he got to skewer, all of them I am sure would be somewhere else.

I have not hunted seriously in a long time. Friends have stopped phoning me to go out. I do not know at this moment when or how much I will hunt again.

This is some of my story about how and why I hunted, long ago.

1

I suppose the very first animal I saw killed and in the back
of a truck was a bull moose, sometime in the early 1950s.
The blacksmith who lived next door to us on Blanche
Street shot it. My father at that time went hunting every
year—and it caused much excitement when he left, and
came back. I remember seeing his rifle standing in the hall-
way between the kitchen and living room. The fact that
you needed to be strong to carry it around gave it credibil-
ity. And we knew instinctively that it was his rifle and not
ours to touch.

He was a deer hunter mainly (he shot a deer on the day
I was born, October 17, 1950). After a time, as it does with
most people, hunting became a thing of his youth, and he
put his rifle away, about the time I shot my first deer.

The men next door to us hunted until they were much
older. A woman we knew, up near the first house I lived at,
was a very great hunter. I remember the eight-point buck
she shot. They took a picture of it for the paper with her

standing alongside it. She went hunting mainly with her brother. Sometimes her brother went into the camp by himself for a week with no transportation. She was an unmarried lady, and of course much talking there was about her. But she was a good fisherman and a fine shot with a rifle. My aunt, my mother's youngest sister, hunted birds in the fall. She too was an unmarried woman who lived up on a stretch of the Matapédia. She was away fishing in the spring of the year, and she could tie her own flies. She was not the fisher-person her brothers were, but then again she didn't have to be. She could cast a good line and work a pool well, and she took her own rifle to hunt her own game in the fall, mainly partridge up on the ridges above her house.

All of these people were people of my youth whom I respected a good deal. The woods had secret places that laid the framework of the template of my life. There were here many famous New Brunswick guides, and a grand amount of wisdom about the hunt. But there was, still and all, a good deal of wisdom from those who did not guide, as well. When I was a child, the caribou were a distant memory, a grand animal of the barrens, drifting away like an image in an old photo. Or their racks were in houses I sometimes visited. Distant themselves now.

When I was a child, moose were scarce as well. There was a moratorium on the moose hunt for a number of years, and cow moose were not allowed to be taken. The moose population has grown again, after the 1950s, and they are now hunted on a draw. Most of my friends have been in on a draw at some time or another, and I too have hunted and killed moose. Moose is the extravagant hunt here. You need equipment to hunt, and a crew. It is hard hunting moose on your own. But in many respects it might be the greatest hunting there is on this land.

We now have white-tailed deer, game fowl, moose, and bear. There are also coyotes, lynx, bobcat, and another two animals—though no one lets on either exists—the eastern panther and the eastern cougar. Some see the tawny orange cougar, as I did in Gagetown in 1990, and others see the proud, black, slender panther, as my brother did when fishing with Ken Francis at the Stony Brook stretch a few years ago. Some say they are two different kinds of cats, and others say they are different colours of the same species. I think they are two different cats—a cougar and a panther.

What separates them both from the bobcat or the lynx are their tails, which forestry officials go to extraordinary lengths to deny they have. Because if they do exist it becomes our obligation to protect them. (It is a simple and collective stupidity to deny the obvious.)

The one that ran in front of my truck on a road in the hot July of 1990 was a tawny cat with a long enough tail to separate it from all the bobcat and lynx that made their domiciles here. The pure black cat is, for the old-timers, the true eastern panther, the mythical, wondrous animal that is seen almost as a vision of time gone by, usually by people alone. Peter Baker, a friend of mine, saw one when he was sixteen, standing behind his camp on the Norwest Miramichi. Another hunting acquaintance saw one across the main Miramichi River. My son John saw one last year.

When I was little we could get partridge behind a friend's house, and at times deer could be seen in the ball field just above us. Now, as I write this in my farmhouse in Bartibog, a big buck comes to my apple tree in the front yard while a doe and her fawn are seen grazing. At night, just outside the window beside me, I hear a bear as it meanders up to the fallen apples, filling itself for winter. In the spring here, even now, bears can be trouble. Though few here want to shoot them, there are small children and hidden pathways that run to the river, so early on in spring it is sometimes safer to carry a gun down to the frozen beach.

Bears are to me the most problematic species. There is no reason to hunt them unless they are a bother to people. In the spring of this year—right on my lane, which I can see from my window—a huge she-bear with two small cubs meandered day in and day out. The fellow below me, nearer the water, was frightened for his dogs and thought of shooting them. But the bears won't bother the dogs unless provoked.

Usually when I saw bears when I was young they had already met their demise at the hands of a hunter. I have a picture of a bear and three cubs taken in the early 1960s, and for some reason I never agree to it. If we needed or had a taste for bear meat it would be different. But I am not so certain that many of us have a taste for bear.

The main hunt here is deer, and deer brought the tick that almost took care of the moose. It is a way for the smaller animal to survive. But now the moose population is relatively healthy, and so too is the white-tailed deer. The white-tailed deer have been here a comparatively short time. The first one shot in New Brunswick was taken, I think, in 1884—mistaken for a caribou. This is the northern extreme of the white-tail range—their numbers are far greater farther south, but the deer here tend to be bigger and probably tougher than their brothers and sisters in Pennsylvania or Virginia.

I was sixteen and in the woods on a logging road. It was the fall of 1966. The twilight had come, a flush of scattered red over the trees on my left; trees naked and subdued by approaching night, and the smell of snow clouds from the northeast. There was the smell of deer here, too—not an exceptional claim made by anyone who has spent some time in the wild.

I had borrowed my father's car, ostensibly to visit a friend, and had come to hunt partridge in the place I knew. I had snuck rifles into the woods from the time I was fourteen. I couldn't help myself. It was here where I felt most alive, and for years this feeling complemented every trip into the woods I took.

The fields, with their pit props and eight-foot or four-foot-length pulp, stretching for acres, and then the woods itself, with trails leading to brooks and brooks leading on down to rivers. The smell of deer on fallen leaves that came to you in the cooling wind of autumn—the greatest of Canadian seasons.

That day, I had a peep-sight single-shot .22, which my father had bought when he was sixteen, carried in my right hand with the barrel down. It was a nice little rifle, with the sights so refined that just the glint of the front sight at the bottom of the peep could take a bird's head off at fifty yards. I was using .22 long shells, which my father insisted, and rightly so, was a waste of money for partridge.

Over on my right beyond the darker spruce I could hear the water, succumbing to the night itself. I knew there was an island in the middle of that water, for I had been here a number of times fishing trout in the summer. Since the early summer I had wanted to hunt here, because of the gravel along the roads and the stands of birch trees. I soon spotted the partridge I was after, in a tree some distance away. I left the road, got as close to it as I dared, and, raising my rifle, I fired, and it plummeted to the ground without a sound.

I listened for a moment to the approaching night, and the sound of the shot. Smelled the powder fading away into the twilight. The air had a sweet scent to it, of musk and rut trials, and there was a loneliness to it; and in all the world there is nothing that can measure the kind of solitude one feels from this peculiar scent in the woods at twilight— it is sanctifying, and no matter how deep the woods, it is never savage, but primal. Even then I knew that "savage" is a name applied in principle by those who believe they are not—that is, the word "savage" never seems to apply to oneself, unless in some kind of mockery. I knew this before I was sixteen, and though it was a peculiar kind of knowledge to have, it would, in years to come, measure my acceptance by and tolerance for others. It was the beginning, even though I did not know this, of a lifelong balancing act and debate, between those who dictate what nature holds for us, and those who know what nature is.

Rousseau used the phrase "Noble Savage" to imply a grace that his own class of men did not need. At least in Paris, before the revolution. But it was not used by Rousseau as a compliment (even if he, and others, thought so). It was, in all its grandiose urbanity, an assumption that lesser men were worthy of the application.

The First Nations could be savage, then, but in a way Rousseau felt they were not, as he was, human beings.

My ideas of the savage land have led to this conclusion. Still, it implies one truism: the natural world is a world populated with danger, and a struggle for life and death. That does not mean we should exclude any other "type of life" in this assessment. Here the struggle is more marked. If you break an ankle in here, or down in there—or up on the Souwest, or on the north branch of the Sovogle—and if you are alone, and if no one knows that you have come into this wild place, you are almost certainly in a bad spot. Hunters know this. So do fishermen.

That twilight day years ago when I was still in school, I looked into the birch stands for the partridge that had lifted themselves from the ground at twilight and I soon had two birds.

The partridge were both birch partridge, not the coarser and less appetizing and ganglier spruce. Their feathers were soft, their heads graceful. Those little places of sanctuary did not afford them protection, and I always felt bad about that.

I was off the road about seventy yards when I shot them, and came back out to find that I was at a fork in the muddy, silent road.

The logging road was filled with dark ruts and stilled autumn water. The coming of winter, all right. I did not know the woods as my ancestors had, nor would I. Hell, half my uncles spent the first part of their lives in woods that most people would consider complete wilderness, and were sent on missions when thirteen or fourteen that perhaps one boy in five hundred could accomplish today. Some would think a house five miles away was a community. I am not diminishing the boys of today for not being able to do this—but I refuse to diminish my uncles for the prowess they possessed.

I carried the birds by the feet, quite content in my accomplishment but also realizing that I was here through half-forgotten instinct more than need—the instinct that drove me into the woods (and still does) once the air freshened and the cool nights came. That is, each year the pilgrimage I make to hunt is one I take very seriously. It is not a game, or a sport, really. It is more than either if done right. It is a way of life.

So there is only one way to do it right and a thousand ways to do it wrong. You might start by knowing something about the land and the animals you are hunting.

The first of my ancestors arrived here in 1705, and I have an ancestor who was the first white woman born on the Gaspé at that same time. The links to this world, on both sides of my family, are long. A little later on, in 1746, relatives of that woman born on the Gaspé came over after the Battle of Culloden, and in 1847 other ancestors, my Irish ones, came drifting up the river during the potato famine. My wife's family came perhaps on the very same vessel that brought my Irish ancestors. Her great-great-grandfather lived in a cave up along the Bartibog that first winter, and made do with hunting.

My people on the Gaspé were farmers and woodsmen

and seamen. One of my great-great-uncles operated a schooner and traded in the Gulf of St. Lawrence, another bootlegged rum. They hunted caribou and bear, moose in the fall. They fished for salmon and planted out gardens. Getting to town was an occasion three or four times a year. Even when I was a boy my grandmother would go months between visits to places that had sidewalks.

My uncles on my mother's side went into the woods to work from the time they were ten years old. I say this to show that my affiliation, my heritage, runs back three centuries now, and most of my ancestors have depended, in one way or another, on the land for their welfare and survival. They have been historians, and writers, painters, and professional men as well. My father was honorary chief of two reserves, and I have First Nations nieces and nephews.

We are the first generation in my family to have anything more than high school education, and before us only a few had that. But we might realize that Prince Charles was the first of the Windsors to receive a B.A.

At first, most of the educated in our family were women, as education was always thought of as domestic, and somehow attached to the Bible. The idea of a man having an education when he had arms and a back was slightly preposterous—to the women as well as, or more so than, the men. If you didn't have two good arms, how could you work a farm? That is, the women took the idea of a strong man very seriously. The inclination to think that women were looking for education and ideas in a man is a notion born of the last generation, the first that went to university in any number, many of whom gave up everything to do with their parents and grandparents. Only lately have they started, in late middle age, to drift back to what they relinquished. (The back-to-the-landers, I will later show, are a different case.)

My paternal grandfather came with a degree in music from the London Conservatory. But before he died of diabetes, he had his own hunting and fishing lodge, and he was both an entertainer and a woodsman. In fact, most woodsmen are entertainers in one way or the other.

My mother's father, a proud Scot, worked until he died; my grandmother was still doing a hard day's work when she was eighty-five, and questioning me about Churchill's reckless gamble in 1915 to try and take Constantinople. Their lives were as expansive and as hard as that of anyone who ever went to the gold rush, or travelled across the prairies by horse.

It was still this way when I became old enough to hunt. In some sections of our country it is this way still. What is wrong with this? Absolutely nothing. Of course I have written about it enough to know that some tend to make light of it.

"I have no desire to shoot a moose," said a professor from Ottawa I once knew, offering the voice of definitive wisdom in the argument (which means that anyone really knowing enough about it, knowing how to do it enough to actually write about it, would be sanctioned and condemned as well).

I might have told him that a butcher's hands were over the blood of the steak he was then enjoying.

Intellectuals believe they have the answers to all of today's questions, well thought out. They are diplomatic in front of their own kind. So there is an unspoken lessening of one's humanity the farther you get from the intellectual centre, and I know people as far away from the intellectual centre as you could imagine.

So then many of my professor's rank have ceded fishing as a benign and enlightened and intellectual pursuit of well-thinking, hearty, and well-meaning fellows, who might spout Yeats if afforded the time (of course not commercial fishermen), and made hunting a pariah worse than dogs of war. But in many respects they are exactly the same kind of pursuit. Between hunting and fishing there is a difference not of kind, but of degree, as Mortimer Adler would tell us. The pastoral intellectualization of fishing will do nothing to change that fact.

It seems this relegation is allowed without much reflection, even by some men I admire. My idea is that if you ban one activity, ban the other. If we are not willing to do this, one shouldn't immediately put more value on a white-tailed deer than on a fifteen-pound salmon.

I was on high ground that day years ago, and the wind had stiffened, and I was walking back toward the car when I heard the crack of a branch on my right.

I turn and see a young buck (I think about a four-pointer) rushing out toward me, not even caring that I am there. At the very last instant he changes direction. Very startled, I hold my rifle up in protection, thinking he is going to rush into me. But he turns slightly, and bounds across the road in one leap and is gone in the tangle toward the river, and once again I am alone. The evening darkness and smell of fall and the soundless beauty of the darkening autumn world surround us both. He came out of the bush and at me so quickly it seems as if I was dreaming it.

I am young but I am not foolish enough to turn my sights on him with a .22-calibre single-shot rifle at dark. So I simply stand where I am, on a slope toward my car in the approaching night, and watch him disappear. It is a startling, moving moment.

I wonder, though, why he was in such a hurry. Perhaps there was another hunter on the old overgrown road that this one intersected somewhere beneath my car. Perhaps the deer caught this hunter's scent and turned and ran across in front of me.

Deer seem somehow ethereal and almost phantom-like. One could hunt them for days and not see them, only their hoofprints along a muddy lane, and then all of a sudden in late afternoon they stand before you. Suddenly they loom large in front of you when you least expect it.

The old logging road is now part of a highway going off to other places, and the animals have been pushed farther away. That little buck might have lasted into that winter or he might not have. There were three weeks of hunting season left, so his chances rose slightly with each passing day. But with each passing day, more hunters would come to make their claims, and the air would be crowded with the subtle scent of rifle fire. So it was an uneasy tradeoff. The number of hunters and weather in the hunt's favour rose exponentially with the passing of time. The snow would come, as it did a day or two later, so he would be easier to track. (But only the best hunters, sure of them-selves and the woods, would track him with success, for getting lost in the woods while tracking is easy.) There was also his predilection at this time of year for making his scrapes and coming back in a rather obvious circle to check them, to see if a doe had come by and left her urine—which meant a chance at mating. Bucks become more insensible as their desire to rut crowds out everything else. They are not unlike humans in this regard. So any half-decent hunter can sit on a trail, or just off a trail, and wait.

If the buck lived he would likely have a bigger rack next year with more tines, be twenty or twenty-five pounds stronger. This would make him more of a target to some. For big deer, like big moose, are a prize, which makes the theory of "survival of the fittest" somewhat suspect and duplicitous. That is, what the deer would grow to protect him from any other predator would not protect him from the weakest of men with a rifle. In fact, he would finely fit into a category called "the big buck"—the legendary animal that all hunters, good or bad, young or old, hunt. That you go out with your father to hunt as a youngster, and the vision of which remains in your blood a lifetime. By his very nature, this big animal is a target and a symbol and a scapegoat all at the same time. A lord no longer a lord but a prize, like a doomed prince in a besieged castle. The trouble, for hunters at any rate, is that he is oftentimes smarter than that mythical prince. Deer have gotten away from a half dozen hunters in one day. Their scrapes, their tracks, and droppings are fresh in newly fallen snow, and through the muted numbing woods they are heard. But suddenly they stop, wait, and then move again, off in a direction not anticipated, and as silently as shadow slip away.

Cold, night dark, food scarce, coydogs, lynx, and eastern panther (as I say, it still exists), yet they are tenacious in their God-given ability to survive. Deer qualify as one of the toughest animals in the world.

I do not know what happened to that buck I saw forty-five years ago, but I can estimate fairly that it lasted only a year or two longer at the most, which would give it four years in the world. And four years in the world its way (as so many men and women know) is better than ten in the world where you play toady or trained seal.

At any rate, that deer, that buck I saw when I was sixteen, went off to an uncertain future, and so did I. It might have ended that year, or the next—if not, certainly no later than the next after. He might have been shot, or died in winter—though deer are as tough an animal as there is, able to withstand temperatures dropping to minus-forty, and gales and blizzards sweeping in off the Northumberland Strait. But some way or another it would have met its end, somewhere in those deep woods, when I was still a boy, when all those paths led some-where mysterious and earthen. The last thing it might have seen was a grader along the road, or a backhoe that moved into that section in 1967. Its eyes might have witnessed the change of its very world, without under-standing why.

By the time I was fifteen I had stayed in camps in January and slept in the open woods in winter with my friends. I knew how to fire a rifle and was a fair shot—actually, a fairly good shot. These were the credentials of most of my friends, and probably tons of kids across our coun-try. At that time I hunted partridge, and unfortunately

(I regret this very much) one or two porcupines. And over time I became a better hunter than I was a fisherman.

I thought of this on our way home this fall. Snow came over the Plaster Rock Highway, and all the way along that secluded road I was looking into the hardwood ridges and back bogs for deer and moose. Making a bet with my younger son, Anton, I told him I could stop the car and find a fresh deer track within two hundred yards. It was an easy bet. The tracks had to be fresh because the snow had just fallen.

As boys (and many girls) most of us fished in the summer—those short, hot months of growth, when blueberries thickened in the hot, still blueness of afternoon. And after, when the ground cooled, and the wind became thinner and the days short, with clear blue autumn skies, we, or those we knew, took up our rifles and went hunting. School, cramped as we were in the baby boom generation, was an agony.

The woods told us everything we needed to know about what was important. There isn't a boy I grew up with who wouldn't have given up a high mark in math for a buck deer. (Well, maybe one or two.)

Now as a man of sixty I go into the woods, along the northwest Miramichi in late summer, and smell musk and snow in the drafts through the dark trees, even after the full moon in late July. I will think of hunting. If I am fishing up on the Black Rapids, on the main Souwest, or far off Disappointment Pool on the south branch of the Sovogle, it is in me now as it was always. I cannot imagine a time when it wouldn't or couldn't be—even if I hunt less and less every year.

I have come to Toronto to live, and live unsettled among the urban souls, in a literary world I have never been comfortable in and more often than not have been excluded from. Travelling outside of Toronto, on autumn nights I still search fields that have remained untamed—see hawks in the sky, hold on to the smell of winter as I hug the highway. I can still spot an animal fairly quickly, for I have grown up doing so. In among the ravines I catch a shadow and see a scrawny coyote move across the road, in the middle of the city, whose shouts and sounds, as Lowry said about cities, remind one of the "unbandaging of great giants in agony." I look at the ravines along the Don Valley and Don River, floating diluted with stink and foulness, and know that they were once as pristine as my Miramichi as a boy. In autumn in the city after the leaves have fallen, we are reminded, by the false fronts and dark alleys and neon signs expostulating our greed, that anywhere man goes he makes into self-mockery. The woods, too, if he stays there long enough.

I see my boys sleeping and realize they have become city-dwellers. Once, coming back to New Brunswick on October 17, we went through the Plaster Rock at midnight. It is a road eighty miles long through the centre of our province. The trees hug the highway and make driving nerve-wracking. One-third of the way along, a young bull moose, about three years old, was standing broadside. Of course it would not get off the road, even though I turned off my lights and shut off the car, waiting in the complete silence and darkness. Four times I shut my lights off and waited only to turn them on again, and see the moose, with its shiny black coat and large hump, looking at me. Finally it turned and began to walk up the highway as I crept up behind it, with my lights out. Reaching its back quarter I suddenly turned the lights on and tramped on the gas. It was the only way I knew to get around it. Turning the lights on startled it so much that it reared up like a horse on its hind legs as we went by. My children were ecstatic. They had seen the animal up close. In Toronto they see them made of fibreglass, at different places in town.

The Maritimes, New Brunswick in particular, are like nowhere else. Isolated we might have been, in snow and camaraderie I have rarely seen elsewhere. No dense cities or long prairie walks, we were creatures of the woods and furious streams, of houses cut close to country lanes, within the smell and protection of the sea.

Once, driving a young Saskatchewan man downriver, he became literally terrified because the road was so winding and the trees were so close.

Most people I knew fished in the summer, hunted in the fall. For anyone I knew, this was as natural a way of life as could be imagined. When I come back here in the fall, I realize how much tradition has a hold over us. There is still in my blood that desire to go on a moose hunt, or get my deer rifle out. I make phone calls, as I did when I was home last week, to ask who has lucked in this year. My brother-in-law tells me there is a large buck behind his wood cut, and along my own land I have seen three doe. While down on the shore, my wife's cousin's husband has seen an eastern panther once again, walking along his road on a cold autumn day. So black it was, he believed at first it was the bear he had seen in spring, but then he realized it was no bear.

It is even better that no official voice will say they still exist.

———

I went out to the car that day I was sixteen and hunting partridge, and the wind had picked up, and the ground had turned cold, the smell of cooling mud in autumn twilight. I would take the breasts of the birds I had shot home to my mother, who loved partridge, having grown up in the wilds of Matapédia as a child. In fact, her world was much rougher than the world I knew. Beside her house, on the hill, was a summer home of the actor Walter Pidgeon, who was originally from Saint John, and who built his place in the wilds of Canada. My brothers and I, as children, used to play there, running around his veranda and leaning against his log cabin walls, looking in his windows to see a caribou head mounted over the fireplace. Whether Mr. Pidgeon took this caribou or not, I do not know. Called back one day by my mother from her veranda, my brother and I saw our first deer, standing in the gloom of afternoon, by the family brook.

That day I got back to the car, the evening sun had fallen down behind the hemlock and spruce, and I realized that I was in serious woods—not the little jack pine and stumped cuts of local loggers. I'd needed a car to come this far up the road, and for the first time I realized what it was like to be alone. Besides, the back tire was flat.

So this was my first test as a hunter. And it had nothing to do with hunting. Or, in a way, I suppose it had everything to do with it.

Our machines have made hunting less than it once was, and perhaps less than it was intended to be, but still, if done right, there is something noble in its design.

That my great-uncle when he was sixteen shot a moose

where the high school now is in our hometown meant he was able to walk to his game. He grew up close enough to the industry and husbandry of animals that he could tell a pig from a goat. With our modern advancements children know (or we assume they do) the different kinds of dinosaurs, and winged reptiles of ancient millennia, but have nothing to measure the farm that still must sustain them.

I suppose nothing tells us this more than a city.

There are many who have never seen woods telling us we have no right to go into one, while they walk over city sidewalks, each block of which has destroyed ten thousand animals. That is perhaps the highest compliment vice pays to virtue.

2

It was sometime in the 1920s when my Uncle Richard, being very young, was given a task one late September. His father, Hudson, my grandfather, was away guiding richer men to moose far to the north, on the Gaspé, against the background of a river where they had scouted earlier in the year. They had gone in with backpacks and mule, past the place where my grandfather hauled lumber for one of the lumber barons there, and it was deep woods beyond, heavy hemlock and spruce, and frothy bunting streams that roared down from the mountains into the green waters of the Matapédia, hills and wilds that no one had ever been to, streams that made endless rainbows as they cascaded down, rainbows for the world that no human saw. Even now the Matapédia and Miramichi are so obscure that most people could not point to them on a map—though great men come to fish and hunt in both. In fact, there is one encyclopedia I own that has three pages on Al Capone, and three paragraphs on Canada.

Back then, less than a hundred years ago, there were places where, at any given moment as you walked, yours might have been the first human foot to have touched. It is possible that it is still that way now in some spots along our great rivers of the east. In fact I am sure it must be, that I myself stepped, in the golden days of my youth, where no one else ever had.

If my uncle didn't know that, he knew much else. Once I asked one of his brothers—a man whose hands were three times the size of mine, and who had been perpetually whipped in school because he was left-handed—how long was the canoe he had lying up against the barn. Never having learned feet or inches, words or numbers, he thought a second and then, spitting his tobacco, said, "Well, boy— she's long enough, I guess."

That, my son, is genius.

His brother had it too. He had to have. With children at home and hardship in living where they did, he took on a man's job along the Matapédia from the time he was ten. He guided fishermen up from New York or Rhode Island in the spring and summer and went to work for the lumber company when he was twelve.

Now he was going through the woods to find his father, with little idea of how to get exactly where he must, yet prodded forward by his mother's words:

"Bring your father here, now."

If at all possible he could do no less. The woods were dense, the rapids strong, the nights turning cool, and he was not more than a boy. The woods very often are more like a living, breathing obstacle course, where windfalls and intractable ground hamper your progress and make necessary so many detours that it is easy to confound your way.

He had never been that far into the real woods—the great woods, as Faulkner reminds us in "The Bear," the deep woods that weave and knit against the hills of our rivers and swallow us whole. That is, at the time, ten yards from a beaten path and he would have remained unseen.

But he walked in the general direction, and forded small, swift streams alive with coloured rocks, and the first fallen leaves, in his heavy pants and corked boots. At noon hour he found himself in an apple orchard and shook the tree, and filled his pockets, and moved quickly off, for the apples were a treat for bear as well, and he knew bear were nearby (now, over his eighty years in the woods he must have met every bear in the neighbourhood at least twice). There were white-tailed deer he saw, just coming into the area and replacing the caribou, and after a time, about supper, he smelled some smoke, and made his way through a cedar swamp, where he noticed a bull moose in a little grove.

His father was in camp, as were the man and boy he was guiding. The "sports" had taken the train up from New York—my uncle had never been on a train. And to him they were people as exotic as from another world. He would not speak to them to interrupt his father or their supper. This was something much more subtle and complicated than "knowing your place." From the time my uncle was a boy, he knew three times as much about the natural world as any man he guided, but he would be loath to say it, knowing they themselves knew things about the world he himself didn't, and to have them here was to their, and not his, disadvantage. He would have expected the same consideration in their territory, one commensurate with the politeness he showed. I often wonder if he ever got it.

By the time he was fifteen he was relied upon by men who might in their world make millions of dollars but knew nothing outside their own offices or their function as businessmen. This is a fact absolute. And he was kindly toward those men. By the time he was twenty he spoke English, French, and Cree, and knew much about the history of all, and took men into the woods who knew nothing of their own history even as their policies tried to rewrite it. But I have more often than not felt sympathy for those men, who rode on trains, or flew in planes, to meet their destiny in the dark woods of New Brunswick.

Now, on this long-ago night my uncle sat on a windfall, drank some water, and ate a piece of bread with corned beef. Finally out of the fractured comments he discovered their situation. It was not an unusual one for sport hunters then or now. In fact, it is one of the things that happen that guides pray will not. In this way, the hunt, at its best, is as much about honour and duty as Achilles's and Sarpedon's position in the Trojan War.

They had brought a moose down, and hadn't found it. The man had shot it just at dark, just after my grandfather had told him not to. (My grandfather could not make that a complaint now, however.) The moose blew wind and blood from his nose, staggered, but did not go down, and in the gloom and growing dark, my grandfather had searched over the terrain but had not come upon it. He had come back to camp and made supper in silence.

The man, who had won a sharp-shooting contest in New Jersey in 1911, was sure he had killed the animal—a fine animal it was, as well, with a massive hump and twenty-four-point rack. But they had not found it, and now the lanterns glowed and the night was growing dark. Small gusts of wind framed the stillness in cooling drifts of air down from Labrador. Snow in a month. The man would be gone in two days. My grandfather would break camp and go in to cut for one of the lumber companies. He would work through the winter in mind-numbing cold, from dawn until dark. Then in spring he would ride the logs on the spring flow, to the mills. But he was not thinking of that at the moment. The only thing he could think of was that he must find the animal, and make sure it was killed.

The man had a fine rifle my uncle had never seen before, with a custom-made engraved stock and a large telescopic sight—the first my Uncle Richard had seen as well. He stared at it a subtle moment without speaking. My grandfather, in his breeches and long-sleeved underwear, was solid muscle at five-foot-ten, and he could lift three times his body weight onto his back. But that did not help him out of this quandary. He did not want the animal to suffer— the situation was "not the best," as he would say at times. He did not want to blame the hunter—especially in front of the man's young son—but he had told him they had done calling and would come back in the morning, for though they had heard the moose approaching, the animal had not come into the clearing as they had wanted, and it was far too dark to be sure of the kill. "She be too late for the long shot," as my grandfather had told him when they'd finally seen the huge creature against the gloom of far-off trees.

The man fired when my grandfather had his back turned, and was picking up his pack to head back to camp. Now he must make the best of the man's bad decision. He had checked for signs in the darkening wood, had found red blood, and was convinced when the man told him the bull had spit blood and staggered that he must have hit it. "Well, we will find it then," he said. But he had not found it. Just once the cow the bull was seeking had bawled, and then silence.

My grandfather had walked downwind to the stream and followed it for half an hour, trying to spot the animal in the growth above him. But it did not work. The trees became darker as silence muted the night. So now the best he could do was find it in the morning. He decided that it must have turned and gone to the cedar swamp. But he was unsure.

Now his son was here. And he was relieved. He was relieved for more than one reason. For my grandfather had learned quite early, at first with alarm and then with joy, that his son was a wondrously able child (although Hudson would never have thought of any of his boys or girls beyond the age of nine or ten as children—which shows the weight at times placed upon not only my uncles but my mother as well, to take care and do chores and help the family). This son could resolve many difficulties by his sheer persistence in deciding to do something about it—a characteristic that would be a benefit to my uncle and many people he had in his care over the next seventy years.

Richard knew three things. He knew that it was the man's eagerness to prove his ability with his ornately crafted and well-scoped rifle, which now leaned against a timber block in the centre of the camp, that had caused him to fire, for a man so proud of his weapon would fire to justify his pride (and since we all carry weapons of various descriptions upon us, we must always realize this). That is, the weapon showed more about the man than the man himself knew. And Richard knew that the boy, who was about his age, was out of his element and upset about what had happened, and for some reason felt his father's unbridled folly was his fault. Hudson would want Richard to speak kindly to him.

And he knew he couldn't mention the reason he had come in until his father had done here what he must do—which was find the moose, kill it if it was not dead, and try to save the meat, for the meat was to be given over to poor families on the peninsula.

He knew all of this in a second, and realized his father was in a jam.

The man, for his part, was angry at the moose for not having dropped dead. As well, he was a little angry at Hudson for not having seen the moose hit. He had also decided that this is how he would play it out. If his guide had been a better guide he would have done a better job. For he himself had done his part—the guide, however, had not realized how well he could shoot and had therefore botched a fine job. But if it had been so fine a job the moose would have gone down. If it had been a noble job the shot wouldn't have been taken in the dark, to buoy hubris up.

These indications left the conversations muted and cold. And Richard understood this, too. There was no handshake or slap on the back, which is what usually happened with a kill. Now to get this handshake or slap on the back might be impossible, but Richard knew that they could get the moose, for he himself had seen it. And he wanted to help his father out of this predicament without letting the man know that he had. So he had to tell his father in quiet that he had seen the moose beyond the hemlock grove down in some cedar, and it was strange that it hadn't moved and was therefore a sick animal.

Hudson immediately gave Richard the credit and told the man and his son to stay at camp and finish their supper and they would go in, he and his boy, with the pack mule and get the animal killed and up, so to save the meat. The man himself was sick of the whole thing and said "Fine," as if to indicate that he was bothered by what his guide had done. Richard and Hudson left the camp with the man's rifle, an axe, rope, a lantern, and Joey the mule, and they made it down into the swale beyond in the pitch-dark. Here, at about 9:30 on that late September night, far back in the time when my mother was a child, long before my wife's own father and mother met, they found the bull, with its great rack of twenty-four points, tangled in the bushes where it had gone down. It had come to life in the Matapédia, with its vast pools of deep green water, in a place like Eden, and had fallen from a bullet that had hit it by chance, and died in the only area and world it ever knew, from a shot by a man who seemed at that instant to know nothing except his own vanity. Had it not been night there might have been a picture of it in some claustrophobic clearing, faded almost grey now with time. These pictures come to me at times through the years, taken by my wife's great-uncles or my own from the 1920s until now. The picture secretly always gives the hunter away. That is, in a second you can tell what type of a hunt it was, if you have any experience with hunting.

It was hard to pack out a thousand-pound animal, and my uncle was just a boy—and he and Hudson worked far into the night to separate the tainted meat from the good for certain families. And the tainted meat was a powerful reminder of the kind of hunt it had become. Far from romantic now.

My uncle's work is a constant reminder of how much boys did in the woods then. Did this boy of thirteen know more than the man who shot the animal? Of course—in almost every way. Did he know it was an unjust shot? A presumptuous one? A misguided one that would set the tempo for the relation between hunter and guide, man and beast? Of course. Did he know also that the descendants of this man might someday look at his own descendants with scorn for celebrating him, Richard, as a great guide, and that in a certain way it is always the descendants of men like this who, as a rule, rule and object to men like my grandfather? Or that the folly of one generation is often visited upon the next in another way—that those in power to hunt will give way to the same type of people in power to stop hunting?

These were questions for another night. This night was a night of working with the head and the hide of the animal. Care must be taken if the man wanted the head mounted. Often that was all they hunted for. The meat some of them couldn't or didn't taste. The tales of bravado were better. This is another kind of departure from what I have come to know hunting was for. When a friend of mine, a good hunter, once asked a great hunter, then in his nineties, if he wanted to be interviewed in the paper about all his exploits—seeing the last of the woodland caribou, being lost in the woods, falling between two bull moose whose racks were locked in battle, guiding men into wilderness for white-tailed deer, crawling deep into logs to finish bear that timid men did not shoot well—he gave a resounding and emphatic no.

"They will think I am bragging just like those hunters always brag," he said.

His words are more important than they might at first seem. He was making a distinction between two kinds of hunters. It is an important distinction. It is the same one made in the movie *The Deer Hunter*, which so many of my university friends hate but which has at the core of its reason the at times unfashionable but still necessary resilient bravery of man. Like Robert De Niro's character, the old man had done it well—why did he need to brag? In fact, bragging lessened it.

When they brought the head and rack out, the man changed his mind. Under the glaring lanterns he became more certain that he had done a wonderful job and had accomplished a successful hunt. In a way he had. He had, after all, shot an animal ten times his size with one bullet at a distance of over three hundred yards. But he had not been absorbed in finding it. In fact, the dereliction of his duty is paramount to the story. That was where his problem lay; someone else found it for him, and in fact he would give the boy a tip. He did not know that the boy had come in to relay to his father a terrible crisis in the family. The boy was too polite to say so until the work at hand was done. But he did mention it in the middle of their work with the bull. His mother and my grandmother were under siege at the house, facing people trying to take the farm, and she had them covered with a shotgun as they hid behind the barn.

Even then, they did not leave until the next morning, after they had fed the "sport" his breakfast. And when they did get out, the cousins who had come to claim my grandparents' place were still cowering where they were, with my ninety-pound grandmother holding a twelve-gauge shotgun on them from the veranda, and the banker trying to reason with her. Saying that in these modern times there was no necessity to become violent when protecting your life's blood.

And as the years passed along, the mighty head, given in its place of honour over the rock fireplace in the man's cottage in Vermont, would become a symbol of the danger he had faced, and the truth would lessen and become unimportant. Over time the straw stuffing would come out; his glass eyes, like a doll's, would seem offended. His son, however, might remember the night and, looking at those glass eyes, be unable to speak of the experience. He would remember the guide and the guide's son, coming in late. He would also remember that his father was uninterested in helping the guide or his young boy find this majestic wounded animal—and that was the real story, that the boy and his father went into the pitch-dark with a lantern to find the downed bull moose. In fact, that was the only story that had a right to be told. But so often we tell the stories we want others to hear. These are the wiles of the human spirit that hunters must be on guard for. For the closer to the hunt we come, the more obligated we are to examine this spirit.

My Uncle Richard did not become famous as a hunting guide, but as time went on he became very famous as a fishing guide. He guided in the green waters of the Matapédia, where my mother had her childhood. And as a man in his old age, his face and reflection, cast in stone and bronze by admirers and artists, show the true spirit of the woodsman. He died a few years back.

3

There was a lack of discipline, by and large unexamined, when I was young. I began to hunt squirrels as a kid, back behind the pulp fields in the woods beyond home. I used a slingshot or a pellet gun. It is something young boys did that they shouldn't do.

We took the tails, saying we were going to sell them for squirrel-tail flies, but at times we didn't, and killing for a while became simply a luxury. I knew tough boys (tougher than most) who could shoot a bird out of the air with a pellet gun. And the first partridge I killed was with a pellet gun, and out of season, when I was fourteen. There were many partridge broods in the dark spruce groves in behind our little cottage along the Miramichi Bay. Most times, of course, we missed completely, which in hindsight is a good thing. In the woods you suddenly became the chief law-giver to yourself. And when you are a kid, certain things are very tempting to do.

Most people I know come of age and grow out of this. There are those who do not, and I have met more than my share. Still, imposing laws against poaching or taking game out of season means little if people cannot or will not regulate themselves.

This is an unconsidered factor in recent stricter laws. The laws have changed in relationship to gun ownership, and rifles have become much more numbingly sanctioned. So much so that law-abiding men and women have not only grumbled and complained but in a real way have faced down these laws, and on occasion have disobeyed them. "The hell with them—I'll shoot everything if they tell me not to," one man once said to me. Of course he did not want to shoot everything. He simply wanted to be able to hunt deer as he once had, and no longer could. Yet this was not such a blind statement—or at least, to be fair, it came from an actual philosophical point. The point was that the government, in its tedious resolution to stop gun crime, was now parenting people with gun laws and registration that were useless to stop anyone who disobeyed laws in the first place. The man's philosophical point was that he would disobey the laws now, when he was law-abiding before, out of principle. He would not register his rifle.

His stance was the strange by-product of laws that are both insincere and useless. The government either does not feel this or know it, or is unconcerned about it. They do not know, or care to know, much about rural life, and they listen to urban concerns about kinds of guns the rural people themselves rarely own. That is not to say that deer rifles have not been used in crime. It is not to say that hunters are not at times willing to use rifles to commit crimes. But I am making a case that most hunters never use a rifle in this way.

The point is not that we shouldn't have laws to regulate guns, the point is that these laws will not regulate in the way the law intends.

Relating this does not make me a champion of the unlawful death of animals. I have always disliked men who have made animals suffer for their peculiar sense of enjoyment, or in rebellion against an unwise law.

I have seen grown men kill animals for sport, chuckling at their own actions like misbehaving children. It is a different breed of human who allows himself to do this. But let me say this: no ban on hunting would stop the cruel misuse of power. And a ban on hunting in a "fair chase" sport would do nothing but stop those men and women who refuse as much as most to be pitiless, while allowing the pitiless to roam in self-proclaimed rebellion against unenforceable laws.

4

I was still very young when I shot my first deer. However, not as young as some.

The year before this hunt I had seen a deer far away in a back field as I was leaving the woods on a raw, cold evening, thinking only about warmth and supper. I was cold and my hands were frozen, in pain. The deer I saw, just a sudden dark spot at the edge of the wood, jumped and flashed its tail and was gone. I was no threat to it. But I patiently waited for the next year.

It was early November—in an age before cellphones, or faxes, when electric typewriters seemed a luxury. I was in the rough-boarded camp attempting one of my first stories, one that I would take and read later on to men, professors, who had come from the States and I suppose back then saw both me and my stories as far more exotic than they do now. I was left in camp by a friend who told me he would be back in a day. (He would berate me most of my life for my books while never bothering to read one. Better,

I suppose, than being berated for books by those who do read them.)

A day and then another went by, and I felt very alone. Each tree, cloud, and knocking of woodpecker was an indication of my profound aloneness at that time, and was enough to prompt my realization that we, as men and women, are both always and never really alone. Camps can accomplish this perception very easily. An old stove has been used for thirty years, and sitting alone you remember the men who once were warmed by it on late November evenings, now gone for good, and the nostalgia that overcomes you is profound. Deep, as well, are the thoughts of people who are far away from you at that moment. As are the old pictures that are taken there—of men, yes, but of game as well, in the bush thirty years before. Of deer standing near brooks a lost age ago, looking quietly toward the camera in soul-felt indifference. It is a sad and memorable piece of nostalgia.

Although I knew my way out, I was obligated to stay for the sake of the man who said he would be back in to collect me. If he travelled back and I was not there it would be something akin to betrayal. However, I really believed, and still do, that he had gone out to see his girlfriend and had forgotten all about me.

Wind had picked up in small gusts, over the outbuildings and the woodpile under its stable. The window at the back of the camp looked out onto a wilderness scene. In the camp was a stuffed moose head, taken by the man's uncle in the 1930s. Perhaps a brother of one of the moose that were tagged and taken off to Newfoundland in the early part of the century. Yes, the moose from Newfoundland came by way of Miramichi. Though they have flourished and grown bigger, with time, than the average Miramichi moose, they are the sons and daughters of moose snared and boxed and taken to Newfoundland by men hired to do so. I often thought it would be a way to reintroduce the woodland caribou to New Brunswick—by way of Newfoundland. But it hasn't happened. And when they tried to bring caribou back to the woods of Maine, the animals died.

Along the road into camp was a cluster of high birch trees where partridge sometimes sat. These birch ran along the camp road out, and then the road picked up again behind the camp. In behind the camp the road became a path and led over the hill to a brook, and then up the other side, through fertile growth where deer travelled most of the year; three or four brooks intersected this one, at various places, all within the next mile, and tamarack and poplar trees grew in abundance. The best way we had found was to wait for the deer to meander down through those poplar growths in late afternoon, though the deer seemed smart enough not to come toward the camp, and it was more to your advantage to get on the downhill slope beyond the camp. There was a grouping of hardwood stands that had grown near a place called Otter Brook, and it was there I was hunting. I had enough knowledge then to know a buck would mark out its territory and travel back and forth in search of doe, but I wasn't as knowledgeable about this as I was to be later on.

The days were turning very cold so deer were on the move, and that certain time of day, from about 3:45 until dark, was the best time to see something. At that time of day the woods stops. There is a sudden silence in the air.

For an hour and a half the woods and everything alive seem to become concentrated. There is a silence in the sky and the ground, and there is a grand expectation in this silence.

I was hunting with a .32 Winchester lever-action, a rifle fine for deer but not moose, and easy to carry and handle. I never used a scope back then, believing it was poor sportsmanship. Now I am wise enough to know it is far more a case of poor eyesight, and I can miss with a scope as easily as anyone else. In fact, the finest shots don't seem to aim as much as point. I realize a lot of people have said this over the years. When the sharpshooter Mr. Boa came to the Miramichi to hunt moose in the 1890s he was able to pick matchsticks off a target board with his pistol without even seeming to look.

The day was cool, and the large leaves had fallen from most of the trees, but it hadn't snowed as yet. That made for difficult travel even on the small roadways. The two hardest things to manoeuvre around silently are crispy leaves and gravel. The small roadway behind the camp was gravel, and off on either side were leaves a foot or so deep. You could be heard for a mile as you walked up that hill to survey the stream on the far side. In fact I cursed every step I took. Finally, at the halfway point up the hill, in among those poplars, I made my decision. It was now 3:30 in the afternoon. I could see seventy-five or a hundred yards through the opening between those trees, to the top of the hill. I knew deer would at times come along the top of the ridge before moving down toward the other side. I was in a blazing orange jacket, which I know is both needed and ridiculous. I had wanted to get nearer to the stream where my sound, if not my smell, would be muted.

But I decided to wait where I was. I would be as silent as I could. In fact, in later years I have found myself standing or sitting silently for four to five hours at a time, without much movement at all, in order to get a shot at a deer.

The day cooled and, moment by moment, became more silent. No longer was there a knocking from the woodpecker, or the call of birds. The wind seemed to die too. The crowns of trees stopped their swaying. It became very still, and I heard someone just off to the side of me. I thought it was my friend, though I hadn't heard his truck. I turned and saw a spike horn buck walking up the hill, fifty yards away. I was surprised at how noisy it was. I had to bring my rifle around and aim and fire, in a single motion. It jumped sideways and fell backwards, tumbling. At first I simply assumed I had missed it. I am sure I was lucky to have been able to down it with a single shot. It was a good size for a spike horn. I spent the rest of the daylight dressing it and hauling it out to the camp, afraid that I had completely botched the job. Later I was to learn that I had not.

I am certain, as I am when fly fishing, that much of the so-called "expertise" of hunting or fishing has nothing to do with the person. It is something beyond our control. For instance, if I had continued on up the hill, as I had initially intended to do, I doubt I would have seen this animal. If my friend had been conscientious enough to have come for me as he'd said he would, I would have been in a half-ton truck the day before, on my way out and back to university. That is, there were a thousand reasons not to be where I was that long-ago November afternoon, and yet I was where I was, just as that young buck was. And I suppose his story, in its own way, was the same. If it had gone to the right, along the road, and then up the hill farther along, as it might have done half the fall, it wouldn't have been seen.

I hung it, took off my bloodied clothes and sat in my sweatpants inside at the table, and ate supper. It grew dark outside.

Far into the night, at about 10:30, I heard my friend's truck approach, and finally saw the lights. (It is strange: in the woods alone, it is easy enough to hear a friend coming and think it might be a stranger.) My friend looked chagrined and ready to take a raking, until he saw my young buck and became certain he had left me here intentionally because he knew I would have the luck I did. He has never given up that absurdity, and I have long since stop questioning him about it.

In the woods, more emphatically perhaps than anywhere else, this is and can be seen as fate, not chance or luck. This is perhaps why so many of the old woodsmen I have talked to over the years believe in fate more than chance. Even if our world has gone on to embrace all the modern conveniences, and we have convinced ourselves that the things we do are managed by ourselves and ourselves alone, that we have become as much at the top of the food chain as the gods we once spoke about, there is a time, upon reflection, when most of us become aware of the fact that we manage very little. It can only take a second for us to realize this. A sudden turbulence while flying is one way to bring attention to this.

That is, none of us has ever been able to predict with certainty the final results of any action we start. Or of a hunting trip we are on. Whether hunting, fishing, or any other activity, so many other factors are involved that our participation is always subject to forces over which we have little control. Or our own nature, which always, in some ways, betrays or surprises us. However, there are certain episodes in the wilderness that do seem pre-ordained. Like the first deer I took, or the first partridge, for that matter.

A young widow hunting moose is a case in point. Her husband never managed to have luck hunting moose, though he had prepared, and scouted the territory, and was adept at calling. Hunting moose was to him, like so many from the Miramichi, the great quest.

Over time this man had come close, but he was killed in a highway accident before he managed to get his moose.

It was his widow who decided to put her name into the draw and go hunting for him. She had never hunted before, and had to take a gun course, and pass a shooting exam. She did, and went out hunting the year after his death, far up on the Renous where her late husband had hunted, asking her brother, who had come in to help her, to stop at the place her husband had last hunted.

Her brother tried to dissuade her, because he hadn't scouted there at all and was hoping to take her toward the lakes ten miles farther in. But she insisted, though she had never hunted or even been there before.

"I am not doing this for me, I am doing this for him," she said.

They set camp late on Wednesday night, in the dark and the rain, and she hardly slept. She was up before dawn, shivering and shaking. It was a gloomy, cloudy day, with rainwater still dripping off the leaves, and the clearing was damp and foggy. Yet at 7:36 on the morning of the first day of the moose hunt, without them even calling, a fourteen-point bull moose came into the clearing where her late husband had called the year before. And though the shot from the .306 put her on her ass, she accomplished for her late husband something he hadn't been able to.

To say this is maudlin and sentimental might be true enough. But to say it is grand and courageous and in a strange way life affirming is true as well. The life-affirming moments of the hunt are moments both elusive and tenacious. No man or woman who ever kills in spite will hold to them. I am not certain how much this is known or regarded now.

5

I think moose have more personality than deer, are more graceful in the wild, more defining of the great northern world. They are the most distinguished of the deer family, heavier than elk and, in their own sublime way, far more majestic, though it is elk that get all the press. To see a gentleman's reading room from early in the last century is to see a bull elk head above the mantel. It proved that this gentleman had enough money to go out west and shoot something that registered to others as a kind of hunting utopia. So people have championed elk as perhaps the greatest of gentlemen's game.

But to call a moose and have the bull answer—or the cow in curiosity appear—is one of the finest feats of a good hunter.

To wait as a giant bull approaches out of the woods, its rack cracking branches of trees so it sounds like .22 bullets exploding, makes anyone's heart race.

To have only three days to accomplish all of this, to have this very limited time to scout out, and kill, and bring the moose out, means for those three days there is constant excitement and movement and worry.

The hunt starts at sunrise on a Thursday morning on or about September 28, and ends on Saturday at dark. Those are the three days. People generally save up holidays to go moose hunting, and arrive in camp sometime on Wednesday afternoon.

They have scouted out their area—but you cannot scout too soon, for fear of the moose moving. Too late, though, and you might be second or third man to a place. Other camps might be set up. There is an unspoken rule that one shouldn't intrude on someone else's territory. However, those hunters who put their names on trees or pieces of wood to signal their ownership are not always welcome. So one has to be cognizant of rules, spoken and unspoken, and of how the moose are behaving.

The September days lately have been too warm, as well, and any warmth discourages movement. Still, moose are killed.

The first moose taken down start arriving at the forest rangers' station to be registered as early as nine o'clock on the first day.

Many people who don't get their moose the first day get agitated, feeling they have missed their chance—especially if other hunters in their area have already been lucky. Sometimes a person will leave a very prime place to go to a poor one, simply because he has talked himself into bolting, and so he spends his hunt in the cab of a truck moving back and forth from one spot to another. Sometimes a man will luck in, even then, and be able to see a moose on the road. Also, people who hardly ever hunt deer will put

in for a moose draw and have little idea of where they are
going. The idea of getting a moose becomes, for some New
Brunswickers, an obligation of citizenship.

Many who hardly go hunting at all will have been in on
a moose hunt at least once. It is a rite of passage, but also
an affirmation of tradition, and a signal that this tradition
is one that is respected by both men and women.

There are other reasons for going. For women, one
reason is to be kind to their husbands by pretending to like
the adventure. To put up with his nonsense. And they do.
However, it seems to me more women go moose hunting
than deer hunting. I mentioned earlier that the deer is looked
upon as the most graceful and wonderful animal, and perhaps more women think that killing them is a crime.
However, the moose isn't afforded this particular dispensa-
tion. It is considered by many people to be clumsy and ugly
(why this is considered by some to be a prerequisite to its
destruction still baffles me). But in all seriousness, the
moose is just as graceful. Still, for whatever reason (and the
size of the animal and the quantity and quality of meat is
certainly one), moose are hunted by many non-hunting
New Brunswickers.

Though there are many experienced hunters in the
woods, there are many others there, at this time of year,
who have rarely fired a rifle. This is actually something
that is looked upon with a good deal of graciousness by the
regular hunter. At times, however, those who do not know
what they are actually doing, or hunting, can make a mess
of things.

"I will tell you how that goes," a friend once told me.
"I had a lad come in, on Sunday before the hunt. He had

not hunted moose before and had rarely hunted deer.
And never hunted deer successfully. He wanted to make
a good impression, which of course is a common mistake,
and something he did not need to do. The thing is, you
can know this in a second. Anyway, I had scouted out a
place near one of the lakes up on the Renous, and I took
him in there Monday morning, to set camp, do a bit of
scouting, and get acquainted with where he would be. I had
a tree stand set up along a good spot. There were moose
there for sure. By Monday night everything was fine. We
had a good camp and had some solid signs of more than one
bull—I had my three-wheeler and rope, an axe and pulley,
and we had sighted in his .306 rifle, before we got to the
area, because he had just bought a new scope.

"'This is the place to be,'" he said, beaming in delight.

"'Yes,'" I told him, "'I think we'll luck out in here.'"

"By Tuesday morning he was telling me how he had heard
that there were great moose on the Bartibog. Yes, I told
him, there were great moose on the Bartibog—and it was a
fine and wild place to hunt, but we were here, and this
was a great place as well. By supper hour that night he was
obsessed with seeing the Bartibog.

"'I would just like to have a look at it,' he said. I told him
we were about fifty miles away, and what was the use of going
all the way downriver to the Bartibog where other hunters
already were? We should concentrate on hunting where we
were. But that did not convince him, and by Wednesday
afternoon we had pulled up stakes and gone down to the
Bartibog River, and on the last day before the hunt tried to
find a place to set camp far in behind the Gum Road. The
next two days we wandered about the Bartibog region from

the Gum Road to Oyster River looking for moose, while hearing shots far away. By Friday night he was certain he would like to go back to our original spot. Now that we had wasted two days and four tanks of gas. So back we went the next morning. Two bulls had been taken fifteen minutes from our campsite, but as you might guess neither one by us."

I have been hunting moose since I was twenty. When I was young, and heard the stories of great deer hunts, I thought that deer hunting was the finest hunting achievement. But after my first moose hunt I changed my mind. For the most part, large moose have no natural predators in the woods here. Of course wolverines did at one time range this far south, and there are stories of wolverines climbing trees and ambushing moose by jumping on their backs. There is an increase in coyote now, and a full-grown male black bear is nothing to fool with. Still, a large, healthy bull moose is pretty formidable. It is wrong-headed to say they are stupid just because they are big enough to ignore you. In fact, many people speak about the moose having an instinct that surpasses that of deer. And if you are in close proximity to a bull moose in rut, they are as dangerous as any animal.

Unlike the caribou, that moved out and were slaughtered away with the encroachment of man, moose show a familiarity with us that allows them a closer proximity.

My good friend Peter McGrath touched a cow moose with the tip of his rod to get it to move along out of a pool, and David Savage touched one with the butt of his gun, when hunting deer.

Although this is true, they are still a very dangerous animal during the rut, which starts at hunting season. My youngest brother, when he was about seventeen, was followed for two miles by a bull moose when he was hunting partridge. The moose stayed parallel to him, just off the woods road, snorting and tossing its head. Finally, as he got close to the camp, the moose broke off at a run, its huge rack tossing up as he crashed back into the woods.

Sometimes one thinks of them as almost human.

In Alden Nowlan's poem "The Great Bull Moose," the moose takes on the quality of humanity, or a Christ figure, or, as some say, Nowlan himself, who at times had a right to feel persecuted. The old bull moose comes down from "the purple mist of trees on the mountain" and is a gigantic solitary figure among the puny mortals who surround and eventually kill him. And although it verges on sentimentality it is a powerful poem, an indictment not so much of hunters as of those who would kill something because of fear. Those who would kill a moose for simple pleasure, or trap or net or snare one, or kill it to sell the meat for profit show the very worst of human nature.

When I was in my early twenties my brother and I went on a moose hunt far up the Little Souwest, into an area neither of us knew well but where we had heard there were great moose. This was the area I had heard about since I was a child. We were sure we would get our moose that long-ago year. It was an area of black spruce and cedar swamp, an area so thick with trees that daylight diminished twenty yards into the woods. Here big moose roamed, far away from man.

Each of us had grown up hunting, had some experience with bird and deer hunting, and my brother knew the woods as well as many his age. But we had not scouted, as we would in later years, and though we thought we did, we didn't have the best rigging. As would be said of many inexperienced moose hunters: "We weren't rigged out." The largeness of the animal did not register, as it would in later hunts. In later hunts everything we didn't do right on this hunt would be taken care of. So this was a learning trip. We carried .303 rifles with 180-grain bullets—bullets both fast and heavy-hitting.

We arrived on the evening before the hunt. The days were hot, which is an unfortunate condition of the time of year the moose hunt is held. We had a stand twenty feet up a bedraggled spruce, and we watched a lonely moose trail from dawn until dark that first day, now and again trying a call that wasn't answered.

Our stand, such as it was, was dangerous—a few boards placed over some branches, with our heads poking through. Any slip from that would result in a fall and perhaps serious injury, or the rifle that we carried in our hands going off. As I said, the young have no special distinction, except being young.

I remember to this day: just after sunup, as we got into the stand, a particular grey, dried-out clump of grass far down the trail near a small shale bank made it look, when it moved in the slight breeze, as if a moose had just stepped onto the trail and was moving toward us. My brother raised his gun to fire—and then put it down, catching on to the illusion. This is far from being a rookie mistake or unusual. In the thick, overgrown trails, a change in the wind can at times make one think something is there that is not. It is, in fact, all a part of the hunt.

On the second day, our uncle (my father's brother) arrived—and he had better knowledge of where to hunt and how to call. He told us to move our position a mile or so, in toward a swampy part of ground, and he began, at intervals of roughly ten minutes, to give the grunting call of a mature bull, which is not only different from the long trail of a cow moose but different, too, from the quick bleat of a young bull.

Late on the second day we had an answer far up the black spruce hill, a bawling of a cow moose, which is the eeriest sound in the forest and makes one think, in those black-shrouded pathways, of the ghosts of old lumbermen. Some say the cow's call is what made our lumbermen believe in ghosts like "the Dungarvan Whooper."

I have never heard anything remotely approaching it, and I cannot describe the chill it first gives you as it comes down to you, reverberating through the old growth of woods:

"Owwwwwwwwhooooooooooooummmph."

Its reverberating quality is what a moose caller tries to produce, with as much authenticity as humanly possible. The reverberation of both the bull and the cow cry is what makes them striking, and it is the woods itself that becomes a part of the fascinating thrill of the call, for the sound echoes and bounces from tree to tree, causing a bellow. At dark, and alone, that bellow is something to hear.

"That's the cow," our uncle said. "The bull will be around tomorrow." That is, we were calling a mature bull call that would attract the female and upset the male. The male would respond to the challenge and come out at us; young bulls might come into the area as well. We went back to the camp, and fried potatoes and bologna, ate back bacon and bread, and sat out on the porch.

But the third day was the hottest day of the hunt. Mosquitoes made their way back and forth from one ear to the other. The heavy jacket I had on, with high boots and Humphrey pants—I was dressed as I would be during late deer season—made me sweat all day. No call was answered, and at dinnertime, when we boiled up some water for tea and watched some spruce partridge walk in and out among some ferns, it looked as if we wouldn't have any luck. My uncle began to tell us stories of other moose hunts he'd been on—how he was chased for a mile one day by a great bull who was in rut. As the day wore on our talk became sparser and more solemn.

At about three o'clock we started up the calls again. My uncle was a good caller. He mightn't have been as grand a caller as the legendary Paul Kingston, or the Micmac who taught us the trick, but he was very fine, especially with the short huff of the bull.

But we didn't get an answer—and three o'clock became four, and it seemed as if our preparedness and our strategy had not paid off. For at times those who are young have little strategy.

The old grown wood stretched out for miles above us, grey and solemn, where now and again in the far-off distance we would hear the sharp report of a .308 or the dull, heavy pack of a .306. This was the wood I had heard about all my life. It was older than I was by 2,000 years, and it looked upon me from its advantage as nothing more than a lonely passerby. It had heard Native boys as young as me

1,200 years before. It had heard the sounds of men in winter stalking game in the year 915.

And all the greatness of these men, and their deep understanding of this world, their songs, traditions, and those they had loved, had now passed away. The moss on the trees became shadowed, and ghostly curtains hung down, blowing a little in a nearly imperceptible breeze that told us we were in a living world, quite independent of who we were.

It was a solitary place, this woods, approaching evening, and we had a long way back to the camp, and then a longer way home.

That is what our minds were settled on ten minutes after our uncle's last call, when suddenly, and seeming only a hundred yards or so away, came the mournful accepting call of the cow.

My brother turned, raised the old army-issue .303 British rifle, undid the safety, and right in front of us, no more than twenty yards away, came a 900-pound sixteen-point bull. He had not called at all. He'd come to the cow, had heard us, and was sure he had a rival. A rival he could make short work of. My brother fired quickly, and he needed to, or one of us might have been dead. What I think of, in retrospect, is Dolokhov's comment on duelling in *War and Peace*. Duelling, he tells young Rostov, is like bear hunting. "Everyone fears a bear . . . but when you see one your fear's all gone, and your only thought is not to let him get away."

A friend related a story to us about a moose hunt back in the early 1990s, when he was scout for a couple who hadn't hunted moose before. They were far down in swamp land off Renous, "a bugger of a place to get a moose out," he related. Finally a call brought out the cow. The cow went down, mortally wounded, and just then the large bull appeared, came out at them. Our friend said:

"We had our moose, and I didn't want to kill him, but I had to ward him off. Sometimes he circled us no more than twenty yards away—blowing steam, his rack seeming to quiver with rage, the hump on his back as shiny as oil. We only had one bullet left. If I had to fire I wanted to make it count, because he'd certainly be able to kill one of us, if not more. I didn't want to unless I had to—so it was a difficult thing. I was with a man and woman who had not been in the woods before—and I understood the bull's rage and did not want to kill it, I felt for it and the cow— but still I had to keep my sports alive."

Finally the bull moved off, and they spent the rest of the day getting their animal out.

You can lose a moose very easily. (By this I mean the meat will be no good.) It is warm and, unlike deer habitat, the moose are farther in, in deeper woods, wet woods as a rule, and harder to get at. Oh, I know many have got their moose on the road—one year my friend Peter shot an eighteen-point bull a mile from his camp. Still, more people have to go farther in than we normally do for deer. They are a much larger animal than deer, and it requires not only men but oftentimes machinery to get them out. (My Indian friend, Micmac hunter Paddy Ward, would sigh at that statement. He has always hunted moose entirely on his own.)

The time of year, late September, makes it imperative that you get them opened and up as soon as possible, to save the meat from being tainted and to ward off the blowflies. The idea, from certain older men, is that it was once much cooler in the late stages of September than it is today. Some days in late September are as warm as August, while in the last few years July has been a cool month. I am not certain how much of this is my imagination. However, I am certain many of my hunting friends complain about it, saying the hunt is set up to disappoint the hunter, and the moose season now starts before the rut— that it might have been good in Septembers in years gone by, but not now.

In earlier times, when there were British garrisons here, people hunted moose later into the year—and caribou, as well. The First Nations people hunted them into the winter months, and could track them down to exhaustion. All of this has changed under law, and in many respects the law's job is to take the animal into consideration before the hunter. For there are cycles in the wilderness, and there have been times when the moose was hunted almost to extinction here—not by the First Nations people but by men in lumber camps a century ago, who used them to feed the lumber crews.

Autumn in Toronto is more mellow and long, and the trees' leaves take their time turning colour and falling away. It is the season of "mellow fruitfulness," as Keats said, and the lights of the houses along the many avenues bathe the sidewalks and alleyways and stores and fruit stands in gold. The pumpkins lie heavy on the steps and porches of mild-mannered people.

In some ways, in a few scattered ways, it is not a good place to be a boy. I suppose I have spurned discipline all my life—at least the kind that is imposed, the kind that says before you even begin a lesson that you are the one at fault. This has become more and more of a Canadian trend when it comes to instructing male children. At least, as I found out, when it comes to certain schoolyards.

In Toronto, I had two young sons going through elementary and middle school who had female teachers at least 80 percent of the time. At first I paid no attention when my older boy would sometimes say that the teacher was sexist. I suppose many people think men are more likely to be sexist, while women try to be fair. Of course in my own life, and in the books I have written, I have always shown that human beings, male or female, can make the exact same mistakes. I also understand the hideous stupidities women have been subjected to—not only my own grandmothers, as cases in point, but girls I grew up with. And, as far as my boys are concerned, I realize too that kids are kids, and will try to get away with what they can. So I discouraged confrontation with teachers, and still do.

My first boy told me at least four times that certain female teachers, in the way they viewed boys and men, and through the novels they demanded be read, were indeed sexist. "Everyone we know back east would be considered a chauvinist or a bigot," he said to me one day, when he refused to write an essay on the radical position of a certain well-known book.

What he was telling me, in grade eleven, was that this attitude was seen as progressive and forward thinking, and young men should realize there was a price to pay.

So, after a time I realized that he, in some respects, was right. I told him to bear it, to get through high school.

He believed there was something terribly wrong in our "fair-minded country."

He is very bright, and he graduated and moved back to the Maritimes before we did.

Once in the Maritimes, my wife and I noticed something. He became himself again. He was no longer in a city—he was no longer a rural child in an urban place. And I suppose that is when I began to realize how much of his young life was changed by our move, for he had a hard time in Toronto, and we probably made matters worse by not seeing what should have been seen—that he was not urban, and he needed the rural woods and rivers in order to belong. And once he came home, he belonged not just to the rural world, but to the world at large. If I caused him problems by moving to the city, I am sorry for them.

My second son, too, mentioned this to me, that some women teachers who had come of age in the 1970s were sexist. Or they treated the boys with more discerning condemnation than the girls. In some ways, there was no way to be a boy. And he began to be scrutinized for being a boy, and put into detention. So he was in detention many times, for many small things: building a snow fort, having a snowball fight, playing football at recess, sliding, and chewing an icicle. Now, it is not too difficult to just forgo all of this and to say that the school and the school board in some way must be right. But in another way, in some other way they are not right at all, and their methods are as puritanical and as draconian as a strap—for most of these activities are the ones boys do automatically and cannot stop.

The persistent idea in our culture was to quiet or expel these urges, because these urges were shocking—you know, wrestling and climbing trees. And how the elementary teachers—and yes, how two of the high school English teachers—taught reflected how they believed males should now act in our culture. And in all ways, as far as I could see, the intention of this was to dampen or redirect the force that pushes young boys to be boys. Because it was seen as not being "fair" to the girls, when 90 percent of the time it had nothing at all to do with the girls. And no girl was put into detention if she did the same thing.

I would not say this if it were not true, and, true or not, I would not mention it if I thought it was a positive thing. But I believe many female teachers in elementary grades are at times one-dimensional when it comes to thinking about children, and attitudes, and what children should think, for they have learned the methodology of equality and must prove it. It does not give boys who act like boys much hope. And my youngest acted like a boy.

This was not just a matter of taking on overt rough-housing and silliness, it was a systematic elimination of what boys need to be natural. I would kiss the book on this.

And so when my sons came home and told me that they had been told guns were bad and hunting was barbaric, and as they came into high school and were given books to study in which men were the only ones who were controlling—I realized we were in a place far, far away from where I had come from.

I realized that the main problem with the teachers was not that they had progressed but that they had never seen or known what they had been taught to hate. That their very categorization was not only wrong but ultimately deceitful. Did I tell my children this? No.

However, I mentioned to one teacher during a meeting that I would be willing to bring a licensed, empty shotgun and rifle to my son's class. I would break them down and put them back together, to show how harmless guns, and most people who own them, are. I would talk about my uncles and show a picture of my aunt who hunted. I would show the articles written on my uncle, considered the greatest salmon guide in the world.

They declined my offer.

And I can say I do not blame anyone for this. But few were ever more certain that others were wrong, and they had the books and degrees in sociology and the right books in CanLit to prove it all.

I believe it was at this time I realized that my race of people, whoever and wherever they were, would become extinct.

A few years after I was with my brother hunting moose, I got my own moose licence in a draw, and called on David Savage, a friend of my fishing days, to come in with me. David has hunted the woods of the Miramichi region since he was a child, and is one of the finest woodsmen I know. He is a guide without being a guide. This is not at all unusual on the Miramichi. I know up to a dozen men who have a similar CV. Which means simply that more people rely upon David, phone him, ask him advice, secure his presence in the deep woods with them than they would almost anyone else, though he does not advertise or call it a business, and he makes no money (or very little) from the venture. In the woods, just as he does in fishing season, he will see that his "sports" (though he never calls them that) are comfortable and happy. And he will do everything he can (this side of the law) to make sure their hunt is a success. He himself, like many others, believes that a hunt can be a success even if one fails to get an animal.

"How can you say you failed? You can reason it out this way," he tells me. "To get into the wood, to have your adrenaline flowing—to have a chance, to be free of the usual structure about your life—that makes it a success. For the three days of a moose hunt, or the week in November you take off to go deer hunting, you have to become someone else—that is, you must rely upon yourself like you have not done before, in an environment that is different from your usual one. Everything you do in the woods that complements this enriches you, and is a success. At any rate, that's the way I look at it."

As I mentioned in my fishing book a few years ago, camps are places that allow for this reacquaintance with our essential nature. They are places that allow one to think of humanity in all its great and tragic character. It is where I first thought of the MacDurmot family in my novel *Blood Ties*, where I first thought of writing the novel about Jerry Bines. And why is this? What is in these woods, along these ancient roads, that allows it? Well, for one thing, we are. We travel roads and old trails that have not seen commerce in a century, and yet we can still see signs, in the overgrown remnants, of our forefathers' hardships—my uncles as young boys working fourteen hours a day, my wife's grandfather guiding hunters up along the old Bartibog in the

1930s. Pictures of bear and deer being taken in the bygone era by men hunting to feed the lumber camps. We treasure it because it is gone now, but its foundation was laid down for us, and wisdom is everywhere.

Of course, there are better hunters than me, and the greatest of the guides—those who lived in the bygone times and guided men like Babe Ruth—may have disappeared. I would never need a guide now—and never did for deer. But few, the Micmac Paddy Ward being one, hunt on their own for moose.

However, there are still great guides. In point of fact, it might not be that the skill of the guides has diminished at all; it might just be that the guiding industry, which flourished back at the beginning of the twentieth century, has gone out of fashion, and famous men and women no longer require the service. Famous men and women no longer make a point of telling their interviewers in New York that "hunting moose in the wilds of Canada was every bit as thrilling as when Bunty and I bagged a rhino in the last true game reserve in South Africa."

The topography of the land changes now in the relative blink of an eye. Places we might once have been able to hunt as familiar territory are no longer there for us in the same way. For our pathways are always being rerouted.

"The road to the river is a mighty long way," as Willie Nelson sings, but many have been bulldozed back, and old-growth forest of mossy black spruce have been lost to the tree harvester. Now three years makes a big difference in the woods of New Brunswick. We cannot be certain—any more than that little buck I met forty years ago—what awaits the woods today. Our companies do not come from here—they come from places as far away as Finland. They couldn't care less for one deer on the upper stretch of the Sovogle. In fact, they know nothing of it. They have never been here. And the Dutch and German families that have moved here for space and adventure have at times, in their singular dismissive nature, cut us off from places we once considered homestead. The Dutch and Germans are the new Euros, and we are like First Nations.

Now there are orange and yellow and red circles painted on trees, to ward off hunters. Just as so much of the fishing has become private, will hunting go this road as well?

In late August of that long-ago year, I came back up to the river (I was living in Fredericton then) and went with David Savage to scout out a place along the main Bartibog River, thirteen miles down the Miramichi from the town of Newcastle. I arrived at my mother-in-law's house on the main Bartibog and met with David the next morning. The region behind my mother-in-law's house is filled with old-growth spruce and wetlands that run all the way down to the Oyster River and beyond. It is a veritable sanctuary for moose. All summer they can be spied from the road-way, at the back of Oyster River in the swampy water. They move off in the fall, into deeper woods behind the Gum Road.

There had been a lot of moose signs that spring and through the summer, and David mentioned that he had seen two young bulls and twin calves and a cow, which generally meant that the moose herd was healthy. He had seen them in the spring of the year just after ice breakup, when he had taken some men far up the Bartibog River in his twenty-two-foot Restigouche canoe to fish for black salmon. There in the haggard trees of spring the young moulting eagle sat perched, a wingspan already longer than its mother's, who glided in the air above almost to those wisping clouds.

Far up on the river, as the ice went out, he often had his first sighting of moose or deer that had wintered in yards beyond us.

"There is a fair population, so we might luck out. When do you take your shooting test?"

"Next week," I said. (*Don't remind me*, I thought.) In years gone by, a shooting test was not required, but because of the moose draw—and because many people who had not used a rifle before applied for the chance—a test was compulsory now. (This test has since been given up because of other qualifying exams, hunter safety courses, and the like.)

We went down toward the river from the Bathurst highway, and came at midmorning to a giant clearout. David told me:

"Just happened—I was up here hunting deer last year and came back this way toward the road, on what I thought was a dirt road all the way, and just at twilight came out on this. So, they have done us in up here a bit. It is like an industry unto itself—a part of mankind hidden from view."

Yes, and in that way something like a crime.

The chop-down was now miles long, and at the edges of the old road there were some signs of moose, but not as much as we'd hoped, and it was also a hard walk to the river. At noon we stopped for lunch, had some chicken sandwiches and some tea, and spoke of strategy. A chop-down was a good place to hunt, but neither David nor I was completely comfortable hunting there for three days.

"This might be okay in a month, it might be great, but—I am thinking if we go down toward the Gum Road and check it out," David said. The Gum Road, named because of the spruce gum woodsmen collected for their kids years before, ran parallel to the Bartibog River up past my wife's ancestral lands, and old-growth forest and swamp still hugged its shores.

That was fine with me. I had seen two moose along the Gum Road the fall before, when I'd gone snowshoeing just after deer season had ended, and it had always been a good place for moose. As we spoke, a small weasel walked onto the birch fall where we were sitting and watched us with happy curiosity, while osprey circled above us in the blue, blue sky. We went toward the Gum Road and checked certain spots, and that afternoon I sighted in my rifle at the gravel pit. I had just bought a scope, and this would be my first time using it. I was not sure if I could get used to it. Added to my concern was the pressure of taking the mandatory shooting test, scheduled for Fredericton the next week. There was added pressure, of course, because people told you how easy it was, and a blind man should be able to pass it with no trouble. The trouble was, at that time my vision was still pretty good. If I failed it I would certainly be a laughingstock. I had always been a fairly good shot (with a few notable exceptions—once when I encountered a whole flock of partridge and missed each and every one). But I was not going to look past the test right now. I told David not to either. I told him I had hunted deer and birds, and took my young hunter's test at fourteen with three bull's eyes, but that still did not matter.

"You'll pass that," he said, to encourage himself as much as me. "I've seen you shoot before—if you can shoot well enough to sight in the rifle you can pass that test." He did, however, tell me of certain men he knew about who had failed the test, regardless of the fact that they were also fine shots.

The next week, when I was back in Fredericton, David went every night after work to the Chatham side of the river and looked at spots he knew in and about the Napan area. I was unfamiliar with this region. The world of the deep woods, to me, was always on my side of the river. But David told me that he knew where moose were, along an old Black River road that he had hunted deer on some few years back. In fact, on three occasions there in the late fall he'd seen huge moose. And as he said, "If you are uncomfortable there we won't go. I find it better to hunt an area you like."

"We need to look over a few places, to be sure," I said. "There always should be a backup area."

I felt most comfortable on the Bartibog, though. It seemed more my territory, and I felt I knew it well enough not to be an interloper upon it.

An interloper is someone who believes a territory is as much his as anyone's. In some respects he or she is right and should be accorded civility, according to the law. But in actual fact, reality does not work that way, for humans are, well, human. If you have hunted on a tract of land close to your own house for years, and have made long journeys in November weather to track deer, you have some reason to think this land is yours. You might not be very civil to someone you view as a stranger on your land.

Nor did I feel comfortable on a land I did not know, because I was always aware that others did, and a man who does not know a piece of land might end up stumbling upon and spoiling another's hunt.

I paced the floor that night because of the mandatory test. Of course I had tried to get out of it by saying I had had my moose licence before (no go), I had already been in on a moose kill (no go), I had hunted since I was two years old (no go).

The test was on the north side of Fredericton, across the Saint John River and behind the forestry building. Now, I knew I was a good shot when alone. With people standing around watching me, that was another matter. Besides, I was certain I had knocked my gun while putting it in the car.

When I arrived there were three people ahead of me, a woman and two men. The target was in fact quite large: four feet by four feet. It was only forty yards away. You had three shots and had to hit it twice. It should have been no problem for anyone familiar with guns. I knew this just by looking at it. Yet people, because they got overexcited or too worked up about hitting it, did miss. In fact, the man who fired before me did. He fired in the kneeling position, two rapid shots from his .308. (How else, I thought, does anyone ever fire a .308 semi-automatic but rapidly?) Looking through the telescope, the forest ranger told him he had missed on the second shot. The man lay down in the prone position and, aiming carefully, fired again. He missed, and therefore wasn't able to hunt moose that year.

I had seen the barrel wobble as he aimed the third time. He tried to make a joke of it but it was devastating for him. The woman came after, with a Browning .308. She made the cut by hitting the target on the second and third shots. The man after her did as well. All these people either kneeled or lay down, for steadiness.

The ranger looked at me and asked if I was ready. I nodded, stepped up to the line with my .303, put a bullet from the clip into the chamber, and fired in the standing position. I brought the bolt-action back, ejected the shell, brought another bullet up, and fired again.

"There you go," the ranger said. "One bull's eye, one on the upper right."

Though I was happy enough to be able to phone David and tell him to get ready, the shot to the upper right bothered me, because I shouldn't have been that far off on back-to-back shots. But I was. The target is essentially set up for a rifle sighted in at a hundred yards; if you can hit a bull's eye at forty-five yards, the sights allow you to hit the same target at a hundred. The trajectory of the bullet leaving the rifle allows this.

At any rate, I had passed. I picked up my moose licence and prepared to go hunting on September 27. I lived in Fredericton at that time, and was Writer in Residence at the university—in fact, it would be my last year in that position. I received about one-eighth the salary of a professor who would teach my work to students.

My wife and I didn't have much money, so a moose would be a good thing for the winter months. I had shot a deer the fall before, and it had kept us in good stead, but the meat of a white-tail is not as good as that of a moose, even though a friend from Newfoundland who had not tasted white-tailed deer before said they gave the finest chops he had ever tasted.

I thought over my hunts in the past. When hunting deer I was becoming familiar with how they moved, and I liked to be alone in the woods—for everyone hunts differently. Moose hunting was in some ways the same, but in certain respects vastly different.

I remembered seeing old pictures of British officers attached to the garrison here hunting in the wilds of New Brunswick in the nineteenth century, with their Mausers and Enfields. There is a cairn here to those boys of the regiments of foot who died and were buried four thousand miles from home. Most of them, the regular soldiers, were very likely akin to the Cockney boys I met when travelling some years ago, with their wobbly smiles and tender hearts. In 1971 a young man named Dennis and I went through a hurricane off the coast of Africa and were the only two on the old ship not to get seasick.

Dennis was much like those ordinary soldiers. They wouldn't have been like the officers I spoke about, who headed into the wilds with baggage and staff. They would have been the youngsters carrying heavy packs who dealt with the First Nations one on one.

I was more out of place in Fredericton in 1987 than I was in the wilds of New Brunswick, for the city was still filled with British and American professors, most of whom did not want to be in Fredericton and complained to their friends in larger centres that their immense talents were being wasted teaching rural barbarians.

The woods was a good place for me to go whenever I got the chance, for many of them frowned on the woods, and on our identification with it.

So going back to it took my mind away from the literary world.

I left in my jeep for the Miramichi waters, and it was a warm afternoon. I dropped in on Peter McGrath and had a cup of tea. He was loading his three-wheeler in his truck to go to his camp. There were two licences there that year, and he and his friend Les Druet would guide. (One year Les carried a disabled gentleman on his back for three days moose hunting—I am not sure if this was the year or not.) I wished Peter good luck on the hunt and went across the river, to Chatham. I got to David's house at about four o'clock and soon saw the company truck coming up the road.

"Warm," he said.

"I know," I answered.

Our first order of business was to decide which one of the three places scouted we should go. David liked the Gum Road, but he worried that there would be too many hunters in along that part of the Bartibog River.

"I think we should stay on this side of the river for the time being," he said, meaning the Miramichi. "Check out that road near Black River—there are still a lot of moose signs there."

"That's fine by me," I said. Though I did not know that

area well—certainly not as well as I knew the Bartibog region—David Savage did.

That night we went to my place on the south shore, just at the mouth of the Miramichi Bay, and barbecued some deer steak, and listened to late-run salmon flip a hundred yards out from the breakwater. We were hoping for cooler temperatures, and listened by radio to a weather report that said it would be sunny and warm in the morning. With that, we went to bed.

The first day of the moose hunt was indeed warm, with temperatures at noon up to about 72 degrees Fahrenheit. I saw a robin hopping along the muddy road near my truck when I took my gun and backpack out in the morning. It was not the best temperature to hunt moose in.

We arrived at the road just about dawn and moved up toward a small, enclosed field in a back wetland about a hundred yards in circumference, where moose had been seen earlier. There were tracks of a large bull there that might have been two or three days old. The grass in this back pasture was about two and a half feet high. The moose, if we were lucky, would enter it with us downwind on the far side.

All that day we waited, and called—both of us calling at various intervals during the day. It was a tedious wait, for there was absolutely no response or sound. Small birds now and again flitted in the row of alders as we ate our lunch of lobster meat and warm tea. Two o'clock gave way to three, and then four. Since we were still on daylight saving time, the extra hour went by very slowly. Finally shadows began to creep through the lonesome wood, and we picked up our calling.

Later in the day David took a walk down toward another side road, to see if he could spot how the moose were travelling. Unfortunately the signs he saw were well over a week old. We called, though, until almost dark. Then I pocketed my bullets and we walked back to the truck in the dark, my hands sweaty—which is never a good sign for hunting.

Out on Highway 11, just before I turned down to my place along the bay, we saw a truck coming back across the main Miramichi with a large bull. I wondered if it was a Bartibog moose. The Bartibog moose were actually quite famous, because of certain guides, like John Connell, and woodsmen who had operated camps there a century or so before. I had heard of the Bartibog as being a place to hunt long before I met my wife and took that river as a second home. I longed to go back there the next day, but I trusted David. He was also from the Bartibog, and he was one of the finest woodsmen I'd had the privilege to hunt and fish with. And he wanted to stay up on that road on Friday.

"I am certain," he said, "there are two bulls there and three or four cows—and that big bull that left the tracks should be still about."

"Fine by me," I said.

We turned in a few hours after dark. I heard the wind blow down over our cottage, coming from the east, and hoped for cold weather. I did not know then, but have come to conclude since, that David took it as a very serious obligation to have me luck in with a chance at a moose. For me, though I was a hunter, and like most hunters I cherished the chance at a shot, it was not overly pressing. That is, I would blame no one if I did or didn't sight one, and certainly not one of the finest hunters I knew.

So I listened to the bay water lap up against the shore, while outside my window I could see the night stars—and count at least a billion of them—and I was content.

We were up before light and set out the second day after a cup of hot coffee. We walked into the same place at daylight, prepared to stay ten or eleven hours. It was a certain feeling I had, that I wouldn't get a moose here. I do not know why I felt this, but I have taken enough fish and deer to know that if one has this feeling it almost always is proven out. I tried to quell it but couldn't. We spoke of fishing—the first year I ran Green Brook with him, a fertile brook that flows well north of the Bathurst highway and runs into the main Bartibog about ten miles from the mouth, and how we lucked in to some very good trout— and how this day, a day we were hunting moose, seemed to be even warmer than those long-ago days in mid-July. We talked about Father Murdock, a famous local priest who lived as a recluse along the Bartibog after being shell-shocked in the Great War. He became a writer of some note, a writer who tried to put the finest spin on life that he could, because he had seen so much death. It was interesting for me to find out that David Savage had read some of these Father Murdock books as a boy, and learned secret spots on the rivers of his youth. David could disappear way up the Bartibog on those far-off July afternoons and return with five or six large sea trout. Some of the pools he relied upon he first learned about from reading Murdock.

Murdock died in 1971, and it was now the 1980s and the world was moving on, changing all things about us.

David spoke of his father, Percy (my wife's uncle), and how adept he was at running Green Brook and Bartibog

River, poling down in a canoe. I also knew that David did this, as a hunter, in the fall of the year—and far from the madding crowd, in the middle of nowhere, he would be able to take a buck. We talked about the olden times—which for us were just before and after the Second World War. The caribou had disappeared, even from the far-away places like Bald Mountain. Years ago the lumber camps had hunters who took too many moose and deer for the men who worked six months in the wilderness. But that was all gone, and so many of those people, and all that they seemed to have worked for, were as distant as ghosts. We were the offspring of those ghosts, still attempting to do the same things.

Many of the men I knew did the same work, essentially. One man I know well, at five-foot-seven and 150 pounds, carried a huge church organ on his back up the eighteen narrow steps of an apartment building without any help. His father and grandfather were even tougher. It was also strange to notice that day, for the hundredth time, that we wore essentially the same kinds of clothes as our forefathers, and if a picture were to be taken of us standing near them, it might be only our rifles that would be recognized as new. In fact, the guides in a picture of a caribou hunt my brother gave me some years back bear a striking resemblance to friends of mine, each of whom I hunted deer with when I was a young man. I will say that most of them would be as comfortable in that world as the guides themselves.

I told David of my brother's moose some years before, which didn't call but came right out at us. It was a strange enough occurrence, and might it happen again? David said that this happened only when the bull knew who was in the vicinity.

I thought of that place far up on the Souwest, and all that had passed since then, so it seemed an eternity away, the memories like the footprints from an old cork boot. Certain spots in the woods—like old trails half overgrown, bridges crossing a spruce barren half a century ago.

In the midst of these short conversations we continued calling. And at about five that afternoon in late September, we heard the short bleat (less than a huff) of a younger bull moose.

"*EEEEEUH.*"

It was some way away, in the large, thick spruce beyond us. I picked up the call and gave the cow call. There was silence, and then the bull answered again.

He called, and a little later we could hear him coming toward us. But the day was darkening. He had to come out soon if we were to get a shot. Our eyes were trained on a small opening between two spruce trees across the wet, dreary field. But he didn't appear. Every now and again, though, we heard him, branches snapped off by his rack, as he came closer.

Crack, *snap*, and then *crack*, *snap* again. Then silence. Ten minutes would go by, and then *snap*, *crack* again. My heart was pounding, my finger on the safety, as we waited. I thought of the deer the year before, along the south branch of the Sovogle, who answered my little doe call but didn't show himself.

This young bull did not come out, and we could only wait, hoping for a sight of him. Then suddenly he stopped, and it seemed as if he was moving away. Perhaps as a young bull he was intimidated, thinking a larger animal was around. Perhaps there was a large bull we didn't hear (although I think this unlikely).

However it was, the young bull began to move away—and farther away. His sounds trailed off until they were almost inaudible, and then silence. Again, night was coming on in soft September, and after a time we could hear him no longer.

It was pitch-black by the time we reached the jeep.

"We're going to change our place to Bartibog," David said. "Two days here is enough. I don't know why that bull didn't come out—but what do you think? Think we should come back, or go across the river?"

I felt this road to be unlucky and so said we would change. Besides, Bartibog had always been lucky for me. We went back to the cottage on the shore. The idea of luck plays a very big part in the lives of hunters.

Early next morning we were up, and after some tea, put the rigging in the truck and headed out toward the Bartibog.

The Bartibog River where it flows into the Miramichi is spectacular in autumn, with the trees beginning to change and the water as calm as a mirror. On these late-September mornings men fall fishing for salmon could be seen across the river on the shoreline. We turned on the Gum Road and went back, with the river on our left, the road still dusty because of the long summer heat.

It is often an unwise thing to do—change your spot after two days. Especially if you have had some sign that moose were there, as we had.

Still, I could not think of hiking up that road again and waiting through the warmth of another September

afternoon. So now it was Saturday morning, the last day of
the hunt. That gave us a few good hours, early or late, for
by mid-morning the moose would likely be done moving
until sometime after three o'clock. As we drove up the
Gum Road, it was already turning light. Everything pointed
to us being out of luck—changing our spot, arriving after
first light, and not knowing if other hunters had been here
before us—which, in all probability, they had. We passed
my wife's grandparents' land, where the Savages had lived
for over a hundred years, coming as they did to New
Brunswick from the Irish potato famine. Each one of the
brothers was a hunter, a guide, and a woodsman.

We stopped a mile farther along. Here the tips of the
trees were just turning orange. When we got out of the jeep,
David asked me if I'd heard something. I hadn't. He listened. I listened, and then shrugged. In fact I felt he was just
saying this to keep my hopes alive. I didn't mind it, but I was
not that naïve, I believed, and felt we would have a long day.

We were going to walk up a narrow woods road to an
old chop-down, and wait.

I loaded my clip into the heavy .303 and walked toward
this chop-down hidden by a vale of black spruce trees, just
as the pink was broadening in the sky. The day was somehow soundless as we took our place behind some small
hedges and looked out over the bleak landscape—which
was in a way, rooted up and tossed, still beautiful. The sun
hit the old roots of torn up trees and gave a splendid pano-
rama—at least to my way of thinking. Perhaps it is the
same kind of thinking that allows one to look at a junkyard
and find an essential beauty still there. Or see a battered,
empty farmhouse as a thing of splendour. The trees in the

distance, about six hundred yards away, shimmered in the early morning, and the clouds were turning from black to grey. Yes, it was beautiful. At any rate, it seemed so to me at that moment.

We might have been there five or ten minutes when David, taking a turn looking through the scope, said, "Here's yer moose."

I raised the sight and looked—a cow, followed by a large bull, was walking about three quarters of the way across the chop-down. Neither of us would have seen them without the scope. And it was a long shot—over four hundred yards. Many hunters I know would have tried to sneak along the edge of the chop-down and try to get closer, or go through the woods. But I didn't. If I had, the unevenness of the ground, and the change of finding myself hemmed in by windfalls and uprooted trees, might have ruined any shot. Besides, I was sure I didn't have a lot of time.

So it was a long shot, but it would be the one chance I had, and I knew it.

I raised the rifle, aimed just over the hump of the bull, and fired. The bull reared, but I knew I had missed him. Both animals started running. I raised and fired again—higher, and missed again. The third shot I aimed a good two feet above the hump and fired. The bull fell forward, got up, and disappeared into the woods.

"I hit it," I said.

"I think you might have," David agreed, but he had no binoculars and wasn't sure.

We went after it, along the chop-down, and searched for twenty minutes or so. We couldn't find it. We came back to the chop-down to try and pick up the trail or some blood.

"Perhaps it just fell off balance," David said.

"No—I hit it."

"It was an awful long shot," David said. And it struck me, how that phrase has been incorporated into our lexicon of slim chances.

"I hit it," I said. But we couldn't find it, and rain began to fall. I was obligated to find the animal if it was wounded. I knew I had to. We stood under some trees as the rain pelted down.

"Do you want to go back out, have a cup of tea—?" David suggested, for he was less certain that I'd hit it. But I knew what I had hit.

I looked over to the far quarter of the chop, where the moose had disappeared.

"I have to take another look. If it's wounded I have to find it. Besides, I am sure I hit it—and I don't want to lose it."

"Then we'll look again," David said.

We went back to the far edge of the chop-down and walked in. Here we could see where the cow had gone down to the left.

Perhaps the bull had not travelled that way.

So as I went in toward where the cow had probably gone, David went in the opposite direction, and moved through an opening between two black spruce.

"Here it is," he said.

It was a thousand-pound, twenty-one-point bull. I had hit it once, with that third shot. It was mortally wounded and could not have lived long. Though I had aimed a good two feet above the large hump on the shoulders, I had hit the animal through the rib cage and into the lungs. The shot was well over four hundred yards. When I was worried about hitting that test target, I never in my life thought I'd have a shot that long.

It took us the rest of the day to get it out. We had to gut it by almost crawling inside it and staking it open. We went out to the highway and got a friend with his skidder to come over the chop. Even then, it took four of us to move it along, where we lifted it onto the back of a half-ton truck. I believe it to have been one of the finest animals taken that year—but I am no Ernest Hemingway. Though I hunt, and enjoy it, and believe that if one eats meat they have a moral obligation to kill that which they eat at least once in their lifetime, I will not brag about killing.

Later that season I went deer hunting, and though I saw five or six deer I never had a good shot, or a real chance, and I decided that this was the way God intended it.

The next season David shot a moose almost at the same place. I was with him on that hunt, and the weather was as warm as I can ever remember. The moose travelled only early, very early in the morning. And again we hunted two hard, long days without seeing anything much. There was more chop-down than the previous year—the woods where my bull had been found wasn't there any more—and we saw no sight or sign (except for a little bat that kept us company in the old box trailer we stayed in). Again we had brought in deer meat from an animal David had killed the year before. He had gotten this nine-point buck along the hills of the Restigouche in the late autumn with the snow down. The steaks were fine, fried over the Coleman stove that long-ago year. There is nothing better to remind you of previous hunts than a Coleman stove. It is a link not only to past hunts but to civilization—and therefore can become a very nostalgic piece of equipment.

At night I barbecued, with onion, a salmon I had taken at B&L Pool that July, and we sat under the stars, as we looked out over the Bartibog River. What did our ancestors think when they first arrived? Alexander MacDonald arrived to this region after the American Revolution. He fell in love with the great Bartibog, and hunted and fished, and farmed, and built himself a huge stone house from the ballast of trading ships. He was five feet, two inches tall, and his wife was four-foot-eleven. They were a small, indomitable couple who had many children, and whose descendants are part of the community still, and are relatives of my wife.

Early on Saturday morning, David shook me awake.

"Get up. I think I heard a moose out near the chop."

It was just growing light but David had been awake awhile, chewing Red Man Plug.

We rose and got to the chop-down at first light. For a moment or two I was sure he was hearing things. When he pointed, I thought he was seeing things. Then it became clear.

Two moose moving off in front of us.

David aimed and fired, and was able to bag his moose, about five hundred yards from where I had shot mine. It was just at light, and I could not see it clearly. Twice David wondered whether he should take the shot, but he could see it through the scope. It, too, was a good-sized animal— and David was using my .303 for its hitting power.

A year later my brother-in-law Edward McIntyre got a twenty-point monstrous bull moose a few miles away, hunting from a tree stand.

The tree stands are usually built at the end of a chop-down or clear-cut—or a swampy hidden meadow. Usually they are fifteen or twenty feet from the ground, and they give a panoramic view. Men call the cow call, and will pour water to make the sound of urine. Some have actual cow moose urine with them. This will attract the bull. One can come from literally miles away, and it may take half the day waiting before it approaches, breaking the branches down as it comes.

In the late nineteenth century there was an actual cow moose, which John Connell had tamed, that was used to call the bull moose out in the fall. It worked nicely until some unknowing fellow, seeing the cow moose, took it to be wild and shot it.

I know three or four men who missed their moose at the chop, also. One person I know shot seven times at a moose standing 150 yards away, and missed it. Another fired at one across the river. Two others left their camp one morning, hungover and wearing sunglasses, carrying their rifles in one hand and bullets in their pocket. They walked toward their tree stand, thinking that no animal would be so impolite as to appear before they got there—and a bull moose stepped out in front of them before they got to it. As you may have guessed, they didn't get it.

In Connell's time, poachers probably decreased the population there by another dozen moose, and there seems no way to stop them. For a poacher to quit he must believe what he is doing is harmful to the animal. And very few poachers believe this. Yet it must be a sickening feeling at certain times for them. The idea of death, even in a legitimate hunt, can still a heart.

I know a man who took two bulls one year, and had one rot. If he cannot see himself that this is wrong, nothing you say will convince him. The more one tries to convince, the more one is turned away with an array of angry logic and stubborn fact—and the persistent implication that you are the one who is weak.

Never being weak is a big thing here. So people should make a concerted effort to understand what weakness is. To look on death or injury without sadness is considered strong, many times by people who have never made a move in their lives without the approval of others. If they only knew what strength of character really means.

Many poachers have an age-old feud or a gripe against someone somewhere in authority. Therefore they are self-justified. Besides, they want to prove themselves to their buddies. That is the real reason for their truancy, and it makes them more dangerous to the moose than any legitimate hunter ever could be. It is a strange thing to say, an anomaly of conscience, but most hunters, most are conservationists. I will guarantee that I am. If not, I would long ago have shot deer from my back doorstep just because I could.

I have taken very few pictures of my moose hunts and have kept very few trophies. The moose horns off the bull I shot are at Peter McGrath's camp up on the Norwest Miramichi. Someday when I am older, though I am no longer young, I will bring them back to this farmhouse where I now sit.

There is an old picture of a doe and fawn somewhere near Rocky Brook—taken perhaps seventy years ago, in shadow along a bar—near where the wind blows in midday, soft, and the ripples of water caress some small boulder. Sometimes I think of such a picture I saw as a boy—up along a river on a quiet day, where the windy green begins to stir just before fall, and the trees trade colour for the paramour they display before dark chill sets, and those quiet places begin to wail and toss in the squalls of winter. I wonder if in fact we ever find those places any more, what happens to them after—and where that picture is now, that once sat on a mantel in some house that is no longer there.

All or most of that life is perhaps now gone. But there came something from that life—an instinct about who can be trusted and who cannot be.

Years ago, Giles and I would borrow Peter Baker's Suzuki 180 to visit our girlfriends downriver. It was as cold as hell, and often we would ride only a mile or so before having to switch to give the driver time to warm up as a passenger. This was in November of 1967. And each of us trusted the other to drive the bike until he was too frozen to bring the clutch in to shift.

So trust came, because it had to be.

We went hunting that year, up to his camp, and then onward to Bald Mountain where his dad, Mike Kenny, shot a nine-point buck just at dusk that night.

That night on the ground we almost froze, the weather as still and as calm as something in the petrified forest, and far below us trees were stunted and bare, looking like the grey ghosts of the Confederacy, while above the stars were sharp as spikes. We had left wilderness at the Kenny camp and travelled to a greater wilderness, where men had hunted caribou a generation or two before, meat for the lumber camps in the woods beyond.

And one autumn day Giles and I took his dad's International truck, and Giles decided to drive in through the woods, over the long wooded bank, to try and find an old road to the river. We had to cut trees and jack it up, moving it forward a foot at a time through most of the afternoon, but we got it down to the river and out to the bridge. When I read *A River Runs Through It*, I realized I had spent my childhood with the same type of men.

I now spend my summers in a farmhouse where two generations ago the road wasn't ploughed in the winter. There are some mementoes of hunting and fishing, portraits of friends standing about a campfire in the snow, with a white-tailed deer up. Antlers from deer I have shot.

My neighbours do not understand me. That I am the fellow who has devoted his life to writing books—they cannot seem to get their head around it. But their hearts are very much the same, and their love extends to me because of my wife, who grew up beside them and is related to many. And I think of many of them like this:

"If people were actually paid for their value, these people of self-reliance would surely be living in the finest houses."

A nice enough woman novelist once told me I shouldn't give too much credit to the working class. I don't—it's just that I refuse to give them less credit than I give anyone else.

I keep waiting for the nights to come cold and bitter so I can go out deer hunting this year. I know there is a buck just beyond the field—I have seen its markings. You know at the very stillest of moments just before dark he will be there.

But now it is November and still warm. So my wife and I can go out on our bikes many nights—she taking the Sportster 883 and I on the Soft Tail. Often the November nights are warm enough to ride along the old Souwest road, or up toward the mines where I saw just last year a cow and beautiful twin calves in downy grey coats cross before me. I still search always for deer.

Most of the families along here have some association with us. They have hunted and fished most of their lives. Most of them I have known from my youth. There are very few of them I wouldn't trust.

There are those I have learned not to trust—at least not to trust with my life. For that is what is at stake when you are in camp or alone.

The woods are like this too—you have to know this before you enter in. There is no way to leave your integrity at the door.

These things have a lot to do with hunting, for a man who is deceitful in small things will have no courage in big matters.

So late last week I sighted my rifle in at the gravel pit. I fired seven shots and hit the small target every time at over a hundred yards—however, the shots weren't in the greatest concentration. Then my son John came home from Woodstock and we headed out toward the hills of the south. My son, whom I carried in my arms through the streets of Sydney, Australia, past ladies of the night who all patted his head for luck, and along the breakwater in Denia,

Spain, during the turbot war in 1995, is now three inches taller than I am, broad-shouldered and fit, and at least as strong as his old man.

He is back where he belongs, in the province of his youth.

Two days ago we travelled south from Fredericton to look for deer. Here is the best deer country in the province.

Yesterday we saw four deer but none were bucks, and a large cow moose came out along the edge of a barren chop where an old moose stand rested against the winter sky. My son climbed it, to look across the barrens and take a look through the scope. (He can climb much better than I can— and used to scare me to death by climbing to the top of our house as a kid.) But he saw nothing as the day got shorter.

Then I walked down toward the stream. Snow had fallen along the hardwood ridge, and I saw a buck's tracks slewed off in the snow. He had been there just a while before—perhaps when my son climbed the stand it had startled him. Who knows, anyway. And the bright day was falling away.

We started to head out, because I knew a road that intersected the stream, and thought that if I could get up on a ridge somewhere in the last hour of daylight he might stumble toward me with his nose to the ground, picking up doe scent—and I remembered the little buck I first shot years and years ago.

But as we drove slowly along toward the upper ridge we came across two First Nations Maliseet hunters, a father and son whose truck had broken down. They were trying to get it started and they were thirty miles from the nearest village. So my son and I were required to stop. We spent the rest of the daylight, or a good part of it, but we couldn't get fire to the engine. So they locked the truck up, and we drove them back in. I suspected, and so did John, that they had a deer hanging—but they probably wouldn't have left the deer, so perhaps a moose down, for as First Nations men they would be still allowed to hunt moose.

At any rate, our hunt was over for the day, but we were obligated to do what we did. And that's all a person can do.

Here and there I still see houses that once belonged to some back-to-the-landers. Most have gone. Those who have stayed are indistinguishable, really, from most of the people they live beside. Others have gone back to where they originated from. And as my son falls asleep on the long drive home, I think of all the earnestness of those people who came here to start a new life, in a new world.

Many years ago I got to know a young woman. Her name was Stevie—she wore granny glasses, and knitted in Uncle Tate's kitchen as the sunlight glanced over the chimes. She was from Toronto, and the man Darren, her mentor and the mentor of the group, came from New York, with four or five other city-dwellers. I have a memory of him looking like Jesus, leaning against Uncle Tate's sink and pouring water out, as if at a baptismal font. From the first, Darren seemed to be the guru in this new paradise. At any rate he spoke of tolerance, while keeping the others in line, dividing up the chores.

They were back-to-the-landers in that age of unrest. They had bought an old house from the family of a man we called Uncle Tate, who had died of a heart attack pushing though a road when he was fifty-four. Uncle Tate had smashed a hospital window and was thrown in jail the night his wife died, because he had tried to pick her up and take her home, as he had promised her. That, too, was trust. And now he too was gone.

Neil Young sang about "a town in north Ontario," and suddenly half my generation wanted to be old, or from a previous generation. A generation that lived off the land, never knowing that even the First Nations themselves wanted, at least in part, to escape from this.

So they came in the summer, this little band; they were going to make a canoe out of bark, fish in the traditional way, plant under the June moon. They had a pocketful of seeds, pocketful of dreams.

"Man, you don't know what you got here—so you better take care of it," Darren said to me the only time I ever spoke to him, pouring out his cup of pure well water. That is, he ordered me to take care of something his own urban culture had reduced to nothing.

They spent October in the yellow trees, cutting and limbing the wood they were to burn, but didn't get it yarded until late and then left it where it was until well after the first storm. After a time they reminded me of a little band of orphans, with nowhere much to go. Stevie's cheeks were often streaked, as if she had just cried. I wondered where she had come from. But she was here now, and in the power of a guru who probably gave orders as relentlessly as any daddy she had run from. I saw her trying to carry wood to the house and stumbling under the weight, as if she were carrying a cross she could neither bear nor understand. It might have been like forcing an Indian woman to go to church in the eighteenth century. The feeling of being displaced must have been almost as strong.

But she continued to carry her wood.

Watching her in those days, I thought of a thousand women who had done the same a century before. Of my mother-in-law, left a widow with nine children at the age of forty-two, a country girl. Of my mother, who grew up in the heart of what any one of these people would have considered the wilderness and did housework from the time she was four. Of my uncle, who, at thirteen, was sent through the woods to find my grandfather, while my grandmother, holding a double-barrelled shotgun, held off a group that was trying to take the property. Of my paternal grandmother, who knocked a cow cold with one punch (a feat not to be equalled by any literary figure in Canada, save Malcolm Lowry).

When it became very cold, Stevie would sit in our corner store for hours, pretending to do crossword puzzles in the daily newspapers. She was hiding from the guru who intimidated her and intellectually bullied her, from the stillness and coldness of the house beyond.

I often saw a look of dull confusion, as if she were a lost Girl Scout. And where, I thought, could she ever go now? Nowhere. Not with winter setting in and no ticket home. Frost clung to the turned-down and twisted grasses; their wood lay yarded as haphazardly as fallen soldiers. There was no way to dispel the cold and no way to get rid of the smoke from their damp maple and birch. No way to make the light stay when it was getting dark, no way to make the chickens look happy, no way to make the barn stand straight again. No one had money for those things. And night—night came at six, at five, at four-thirty.

The locals became interested in helping out, for no better reason (and a damn good reason it was) than that these were people and it was Christmas. And many of my friends who were their age dropped in on them with presents.

They brought deer meat from a buck killed up at Mullin, and moose meat from the first moose we had taken, fifty pounds of potatoes, homemade wine, fresh-grown grass, and other forms of libation. But it became a strange celebration. It reminded me of Tolstoy's quip that at least as much is known in the country as the city, and probably more.

When Darren spoke to us of wanting to build a geodesic dome, he was very surprised to find out that our friend Giles had quit school in grade ten and had built the first dome in New Brunswick, drawing on his own plans and intelligence and reading Buckminster Fuller. He, Darren, had not known that universal ideas were actually universal.

When Darren said he would fish for his food, it was Peter McGrath who brought smoked salmon. Yes, he told Darren, he had taken them on fly, running the river from Little River down to Miner's Camp. He had taken them on butt bugs he had tied himself. No, it was not a big thing—here, take them all.

Yes, we will teach you to hunt and fish—it is no problem, don't ever worry or be afraid to ask!

This was no one-upmanship. The little town was just the land extended. Until I was twenty-four, I could carry my rifle from my house into the woods for a deer hunt. It was not that Darren did not know the land—he did not know himself, and the land simply told him this. Sooner or later the land does.

Life went on. There were chores to be done, by people who had never done chores before. They spoke of sharing, but it was contractual, not emotional. It seemed to me there was more love in the place when Uncle Tate lived alone and fired off his shotgun at his visitors as a joke.

By January there were arguments. That month a young man got a job in town. Another went away—and then another.

I met Stevie coming out along the back road one day. She was carrying a saucepan, with nothing in it. Someone had told her there were winter berries to collect, but she had found none, for there were none. We stood and talked for a moment in the freezing gale of late afternoon.

"We are going to have a really fine farm," she told me. I was so sorry for her at that moment. She had come to womanhood in what kind of city, to feel so left out, like so many of my generation? Cast out, of something. I'm not even sure what. All she had known was concrete. Why had this happened? What sad turning away from her family did she have, in what hot, vacant, urban apartment or house tucked between two asphalt roads? An argument over the war—or a parent trying too hard to buy her love, or loving her too little? Did they even know where she was any more? She was still a child, really.

"So you aren't going home?" I said.

"Oh—no—no!" She smiled. "I'll never go."

It was a victory for her to say this. I might have told her that I knew a family who had arrived at this little place where she was now in 1840, and lived their first winter in a cave about a mile from where we were talking, losing three children. I might have told her that my relatives came over after the Battle of Culloden, and one walked from Pennsylvania in 1805 and settled up on the Norwest. To keep her chin up.

I discovered at that moment that there is something about the land—you look unnatural on it if you are unnatural, you look greedy on it if you are, lazy if you tend to be. If you are frightened of guns or wildlife, the land will inform you. Nervous on the water, the water will let you know. There is no escaping who you are once you are here, on the Miramichi—or anywhere else, for that matter. It is what the First Nations saw of us. It is what I saw of her—she with the saucepan with nothing in it.

In late January another one of them went and got a job. He worked at a garage in Barryville repairing snowmobiles and would come home every night late. He supported this little family of outcasts by doing a job hundreds of men did without complaint, simply because life required that he do it.

Then he found a girl in Neguac and moved out.

So there were only Stevie and her mentor, Darren, left. They were the last. And in that winter, living alone, they found that the dream had somehow disappeared. But what dream was it? I don't think any of them, including Darren, really knew.

Darren left one afternoon, saying he would be back—that he was going into town for supplies. His poncho on a hook in the corner near his leather hat assured Stevie of his return. But he did not come back. She waited by the window, his supper in the warming oven. He had become safe again, when being unsafe was no longer a game.

Stevie stayed by herself, looking out those porch windows, waiting for her friend. She made it until March.

Sometime about St. Patrick's Day I saw her doing her crossword in the corner store. There was a storm outside and everything in the world was white.

She was happy, she said. The wood was drier, and people had made her welcome. She was working two nights a week in this store, selling cigarettes and Tampax. But she needed to take a course, she thought, and come back next year. Next year would be better. The terrible things in the world would be gone. Suddenly she reached up and kissed my forehead and squeezed my hand. She walked on, and I watched her go out of my life. It's been almost thirty years.

The house is gone, and no one waits, and none of them has ever been back. They didn't have much luck. For a while many of us might have believed a new world would come. Perhaps that's what we've all been watching for, whenever we look up at the sky.

I walked beyond Uncle Tate's land late last autumn. There had been two days of snow. I walked toward the hundredth new chop-down that has come since the mill started its new process, and then shut its doors for good. I carried my little Winchester .32—but I have not fired a rifle at a deer in a few years now. I trick myself into hunting by not hunting now. Usually I find a tin can to fire at, sight the rifle in, for next year.

My family—here for over two and a half centuries—is gone from the river, and in the summer the brooks babble to tell me so. My mother died in 1978, my father died ten years ago, and all the children have left. We have gone away, but we do come back. In a sense, once a part of the land, we can never leave. We didn't become peace lovers, but we do love, fiercely, I suppose.

There is no town here now. A city sprawls with lights toward its destiny. The trees are muted and thrashed, as pockets of the forest no longer exist at all.

I walked toward the high ground beyond his house, next to the power lines. The ground was dug up that day, with fresh tracks and scrapes. In one of those tricks of fate I saw the old saucepan Stevie had used to collect her winter berries. It had been tossed up out of the dirt that had buried it for years. I wondered how her life had gone, and if she had ever found the place she wanted.

Then turning toward the chop, I saw a little doe. As I approached she made a heroic attempt to stand. Her left hind leg was caught in a coyote snare, and she was hunkered down beneath the snow and thrashed trees. All around and everywhere I looked the snow and earth had been torn up, where a gigantic battle had raged above Uncle Tate's old farmyard. The night before the buck had stayed, to protect the doe in the snare from the coyotes. And he must have fought like hell. The coyotes—here almost as big as wolves—hadn't been able to get to her. I do not know if the buck lived, but he had done the job given him. Like Uncle Tate with his wife, he didn't know why she was caught up in the way she was. The world had betrayed them both: the snare cynically said that neither of them mattered. Still, the buck fought like a bastard. Never left his poncho on a nail.

I managed to cut the snare. She stood and bolted, cracking the limbs of some birch trees, and was gone, gone into what was left of a world that didn't exist any longer.

6

I know two men who were hunting with an older man up on the Mullin Stream Road a few years ago. The older man shot at a large moose that came into the open. Believing he had missed, and feeling foolish that he had shot at it from such a distance when he had been told to wait—certain that he had made a laughingstock of himself—he wanted to go home, not just back to the camp.

"You can't go," one of the men said. "You have to find your moose."

"I didn't hit it."

"Well, we can't be sure, can we."

Added to this was the sudden arrival of forest rangers asking for licences and interrogating them about why this man had shot right down the highway at an animal. It was a difficult position to be in, and the older man, who had bragged about his years of hunting, was now cast in a bad light. After the rangers had decided that it was a foolhardy more than a criminal act, they left. And when they had he wanted, as quickly as possible, to be gone too. But the two men with him had an obligation to this animal. So the choices we make and must make were played out again. That is, these choices are played out in every office of the world every day of our lives. Sometimes we just forget that they are.

They took the older man to town, left him at his truck, and went back into the woods again. After a night of fitful sleep they got up at dawn and, in a patient fashion, searched the old spruce wood where the cow moose had run. They also searched all through the swampy area where the moose had most likely fled. They spent two days searching and didn't find it. But one of the men, a Micmac friend of ours, was certain, because of the way the animal had turned, that it had been hit. And he was very uncomfortable leaving after two days, though he had to get back home to his own duties as a council elder. The shot should not have been taken in the first place. That the man didn't stay to help them find the moose was neither here nor there—their obligation to the animal in question remained the same. The older man would most likely never hunt again, after such an event.

I know many who have given up hunting because of events such as this. Suddenly the idea comes over them that this is not a game, or a frolic, but a very serious thing. That no one should be glib about the way he hunts, or what he must do if an animal is wounded. The paramount reason for shooting at something is to kill it. That in itself is serious enough to demand an ethical shot. For instance, people I know would never think of leaving a wounded animal.

One year Peter McGrath, guiding an American bow

hunter after bear, had this experience as well. They had built a tree stand over bait—molasses and horseflesh—and were waiting. When the huge male showed, the man fired his arrow deep into its side, and the bear took off. They waited a moment, until the sound of the animal's crashing and thrashing stopped. Then it was my friend's duty to go after the wounded bear. The gentleman hunting it didn't want to, he did not feel it was safe. He was right. It was not safe. So Peter climbed out of the stand and began to hunt for the animal.

Peter was on the ground alone, following a blood trail into a thicket. He would wait for the bear to weaken, yet he didn't want it to suffer, so he wanted to shoot it as quickly as possible. He knew he was in danger doing this, and he knew it was expected of him. It was in the spring, and there was snow on the ground, and the trees were still naked. The bowman could take this carcass home to Pennsylvania and say he had killed a large black bear with a bow in the wilds of New Brunswick (a place, he might say, "way up in Canada").

Well, first Peter had to find the animal and kill it with a .308. This is the kind of play-acting that disassembles the argument for hunting and truly legitimizes the points made by anti-hunting advocates. Peter finally saw the wounded animal and was able to shoot it. They dragged the animal down to the roadside and put it in the back of the truck. It was the last time Peter guided for bear.

"I'm not doing it for them no more," was all he said.

We know that to kill wantonly is cruel, and worse, stupid—but to attack all hunting as being so misses what knowledgeable writers have to say about it.

Again I will mention Alden Nowlan, who grew up in Nova Scotia, and who wrote a poem about hunters and a bear. In his poem he asks us, why would this poor beast's terror and suffering enliven someone? This is a good question to ask those who hunt, and all hunters must recognize this as a valid question, even if the hunt is a legitimate one.

There is a wealth of writing about this topic—the topic of what is cruel and why.

My good friend Eric Trethewey, one of the finest poets I have ever met, grew up as a boy, solitary, in the woods and hills of Nova Scotia over half a century ago. His games in those woods were ones that allowed him to bring meat to the table. He hunted rabbit and deer, trapped beaver in order to get money that was sorely needed—and there was one time when trapping a beaver literally saved his life, for, as he wrote in a brilliant essay, he traded that beaver pelt for a shotgun that saved his family from an attack by a deranged relative that very night.

But even if the concerns about cruelty are at times truly legitimate, Canadians have nevertheless seduced themselves into thinking that anything more than a notional understanding of the subject is barbaric; so their ignorance of hunting conforms to a standard disingenuousness.

In the movie *Surfacing*, based on the novel by Margaret Atwood, the terrible hunter kills a moose, while the compassionate proactive feminist takes him to task for it. What anyone who has ever hunted knows is that this character is not rigged out for hunting, and apparently no one on the film—director and actor included—had the faintest idea of how an animal is hunted or even poached, or at what time of day or year it is accomplished. The scene is almost completely artificial, and yet fulfills the purpose of establishing instant culpability. Compare this to the brilliant hunting literature in Russia (Tolstoy), the United States (Faulkner), or in any other culture where the hunt is allowed to manifest itself as what it is, and one will see how small we have allowed ourselves to become for the sake of an established academic propriety. It is not that I disagree with the scene in *Surfacing*; I simply don't believe it.

Nothing better shows what rural Canada represents or is supposed to represent to those in our cities. The only problem being, rural Canada rarely has a say, no matter how disingenuous these treatises are.

7

In the cold fall we see ducks overhead, or way above us geese. They answer the calls of the hunters, who hide in blinds on the marshy shore. Most of the duck hunters I know will not have dogs; they fetch the geese themselves, sometimes with a spincast rod. In the little blinds it is very cramped, and usually the hunters use larger gauges—twelve or sixteen. They call and wait for the birds to come into range, with their duck calls that sound to me completely artificial, but to the ducks and geese must sound convincing. When the weather is nasty the birds mightn't be too hard to convince; ducks and geese will come off the open water in a storm just like any other animal and find respite in the shallow back waters.

Hunting ducks and geese is more like hunting woodcock than partridge. It is not so easy to hunt a bird on the fly, or to be patient enough sitting in that cramped blind that looked so good in the store window. Some of these store-bought, manufactured blinds are so tight that once you have your hunting vest on they are hard to get down over your shoulder. Of course many people still build their blinds in the same spots for years.

There is more waterfowl hunting along the coast than inland, but inland here is always watery with rivers and islands, so there are waterfowl to hunt. Some days are perfect, with clear, cool weather and a flock of birds coming in on a call. Friends of mine have experienced these days, on occasion. But more often than not, it is wet and cold, and a long time waiting between birds.

The store windows of the outdoor suppliers, like the Bass Pro Shops, which have a huge Outdoor World store off Highway 400 near Toronto, show an idyllic scene. Hunter mannequins are always clean, the faces jovial and clean-shaven, to look virtuous, and the air is filled with ducks. Or the bear is easily spotted up a tree, and the mannequin up a stand is not cold or frostbitten or so tired he is frightened of falling. The deer beneath him is always a buck with a fine rack. The wind does not blow—there is no wind in the willows here. Pictures of trout on inland lakes—with the nineteen-foot Coleman canoe and the fisherman—are idyllic as well.

The Outdoor World off Highway 400, outside of downtown Toronto, is where I go to escape the glass and tall buildings, the miles of concrete. Though it is an Upper Canadian place, I can walk about and think of the Maritimes. I am not fully alive in it, but by God I am more alive.

There is so much "stuff" now—that is the feeling I come away with at times. We are overburdened with "stuff." This means everything from goose calls to chair-warmers to hand-warmers to portable toilets to an array of seemingly useless things for the camping trip you are about to take. If a hunter—especially a hunter from the Maritimes— brought half of this stuff he would be laughed out of the woods, not only by the hunters but by the game itself. We don't need it, it is a burden to us, and its selling point relies on man's desire to be more comfortable "there" than when he is home, and not to succumb to anything in nature that might force him to confront nature itself. It is based also on aspects of man that the outfitter bargains on—his actual fear of the elements themselves, and his constant hope that he can be like everyone else, the worry that accompanies man when he is on his own in the natural world. This "stuff," these commodities, do say one thing, just as a by-product of our instinct. We can gather by all this "stuff" that a good 35 percent of hunters (and it might be more) never see an animal they are hunting—and the failure rate of hunters is high. This is a good thing, actually. Many men I know have never shot a deer, or shot at a deer, or have even seen one. (One man I went hunting with, well into his twenties, came to me to tell me he had seen some deer sign. I went to look and realized it was bear scat. I simply pointed this out in the most diplomatic way I could, and know that I myself have much to learn in the woods.)

I do not wish these men or women bad luck—but I am assured by this that hunting is a very subjective activity. We are emboldened by the activity as much as by the game we seek. If these stores tell us anything, they tell us this. No one should frown at the poor hunter who buys himself too much needless equipment to go and sit on a road where, for three days, he will see nothing more than leaves blowing and trees laid bare. For many, that is what the hunt is, and no one should belittle it. To some it is the finest time they have. The paralyzed man that Les Druet carried on his back for three days is a good case in point. No animal, I think, was taken, and yet Druet gave this gentleman the finest wilderness experience he had had in many years.

And here, too, at these stores there are so many rifles to choose from, so many different weapons that have come along since I was a boy. There are pump-actions and lever-actions and semi-automatics, bolt-actions, .270s, .308s, .306s, etc. All of this is fine, but I have used a .303 with 180-grain bullets since I was nineteen; I bought it for $23.

I have my Winchester lever-action, I have a shotgun, and I own an old 1913 .22-calibre that hasn't been fired since its original owner died in the 1940s. It is the .303 I hunt with most of the time now. I have not fired the Winchester in some years. Last year, at these outfitters, I checked out the price of a reel for a rod I had. The salesman wanted to sell me a nice reel for $730. I told him I was hoping to get one for about $30.

What do we see when we go into these stores but an aching for a time that is no longer ours to hold. That has passed us by, or, to put it more clearly, has bypassed most of us. Most of the men who wander through these places, sometimes for hours on end, are men from outside the city. Although I wouldn't be able to prove it, it is a feeling I have that many here, just as in my early days, are from small towns.

What the store owner or distributor is selling is the past—selling our past back to us, to some of us men who are lost and far from home. A fly tackle shop salesman is overcome when he hears I am from the Miramichi. And

I add to my singularity when I tell someone else that I have shot moose as large as the stuffed one near the rifle stand. (He doesn't believe me, and winks at his lady friend, who doesn't believe me either.)

So many of these things are in the past for me now that I am nostalgic as I look at commodities like the Coleman stoves and lanterns that I remember from times gone by— my father boiling water at nine o'clock for tea, or our first camp long ago at Mile 17 of Mullin Stream. The night of wet snow falling over Davy Lake. (This was named after me by my brothers because I haunted it all one year, going after a buck. I didn't get it, but I managed to get a smaller buck just up the road on the second-last day of the season.)

Most of the equipment, continually updated, has come along since I shot my last deer. This store is here to seduce us, to tell us that the way of life we have dreamed about is still possible; the fake rocks and decoy ducks are presented to us as willing participants in our own imaginary outdoor adventure. Tents, hunting chairs, wilderness camping equipment, and satellite tracking equipment that will enable a man to drive from his suburban home to the wilderness of his choice and be directed at every instant along the way, so he will not have to deal with the wilderness itself.

I am not against any of this, but I am suggesting that many of these things will be bought and rarely if ever used, part of man's unquenchable desire to portray himself to himself as other than he actually is.

Or other than the hunt. I remember freezing half to death for a few ducks in a miserable blind on a cold, bitter day far out on the bay. I am not complaining, I am simply suggesting that this is never a real selling point. Perhaps it doesn't have to be. Most of the men and women there that day probably knew this as well as I. Maybe better. For hunting is still a part of us. We come from the corners of the country to the centre, but it is the corners we still dream of.

Now we can no longer hunt geese or duck with lead pellets in the shells, they have to be steel, and people complain that these do not work as well, do not hit with the same killing power so more geese are left to suffer.

There was a day when my wife's brother went hunting black duck on land owned by his grandfather, with a twelve-gauge shotgun that had once belonged to his father. That is a shotgun that is perhaps older than I am.

It was on the Bartibog where the tide came in, and it was a cloudy, intemperate day. He had arrived at dawn and, sitting on his haunches behind the little tree-coloured plywood blind he had made, he gave a few tentative calls. For a while he saw nothing except a crow or two across the cove, and heard the splash of a muskrat. Soon, though, he saw a few ducks. Then some more. It seemed that they weren't coming to his decoys or his calls. The ducks were coming in high, and sometimes turning away and going in the other direction, so there was no shot. And then they would come in behind him, so he couldn't get the old shotgun raised up, and they'd be off, far above him. It was as if they didn't see his decoys, or worse, as if they saw him and were laughing at his plan.

He kept the gun raised, though, and finally he felled two ducks that came right out from his blind, with the same spray. Down they fell into the cove, some distance away from him, their bodies bobbing on the surface.

Now he wondered how he would retrieve them. He had no dog, and he was not so sure if the water wouldn't be over his head. Some use a spincast fishing rod, and he at times had, but he hadn't brought it with him. He watched his ducks bobbing in the small, cold eddies in the middle of this cove and, hauling his chest-waders up, he took an eight-foot stick with him and entered the water. The cove is a fine place for ducks, but it also has a muddy bottom. He didn't consider this carefully in his worry over retrieving the fowl. He was about twelve feet from them, and realized he couldn't take another step. He was caught up to his thighs in mud. There he was. His eight-foot pole was useless to retrieve the birds, which now floated in toward the opposite shore. That is, the tide was coming in on this back cove, and he was alone, and caught in it. His decoys still bobbed about him, as if to add insult to injury. All this trouble for birds who were now being carried into the reeds opposite him. He realized he would look somewhat ridiculous drowning in this position for two ducks that had made it to dry land without him. The wind blew ripples about him, lapping against his waders, and the day was silent. In fact he struggled in this position for quite a while, and realized he must be master of his own fate, since he was the engineer of his own predicament.

There was only one thing to do. He had to chance kicking his legs up and falling backwards into the water, waders and all. He felt he was strong enough to get himself out, if he didn't become completely immersed in the cove. If he did, and if his waders filled while his head remained under, and his legs caught, he would be as good as dead. He knew this—but there was no rational reason to be cautious. Using the stick to loosen the muck about him, he made a hard backward flop, and his feet came out of the suck. He was able to kick himself away and find a toehold in the firmer soil near those reeds the ducks had floated into.

He was safe, soaking wet, and two ducks richer. It was an experience he would remember, and relate to others, for some years to come.

In the celebrated story "The Ledge," by Lawrence Sargent Hall, a father takes his son and his nephew hunting on Christmas Day out to a tidal island. One of the boys forgets to anchor the boat, and they are all stranded a mile offshore, while the tide envelops them. It is a heartbreaking tale, wonderfully written. I have a friend who told a similar story about his own duck hunting a few years ago.

One October afternoon he told no one where he was going and, seeing black duck on Sheldrake Island, he took his canoe over to have a day hunt. He had his twelve-gauge with him and, leaving his canoe in one place, set out toward the north tip of the island, which looked out toward the cold and seemingly endless Northumberland Strait. It was a blowing day, yet a good day for shooting. The wind blew across the desolate grasses, the implacable sand made hard as granite by wind. Soon he had down three black duck and had wounded a fourth, which he went looking for. At this time he happened to see a small V of geese coming in low overhead, and he managed to shoot one. This left him with the three black duck, a goose, and one duck wounded. During all this time walking about in his chest-waders he never gave a thought to his canoe, and that the tide might catch it with the wind rising the way it was.

He spent some time searching for the wounded duck until he found it, in some grasses, and calling it a day decided to go home. He walked back toward the centre of the island, an island still covered in spruce, with cold yellow sand driven up along the shore and deep withered grasses, an island that sits just at the mouth of the Miramichi Bay about a quarter mile from the mouth of the Bartibog River.

It was getting past twilight, and he was alone, and, as sometimes happens, the wind from the east had picked up and made it almost unbearably cold. When he got back to where he had left his canoe it was no longer there. He kept moving along, thinking that he had left it some other place. But he finally realized that the tide must have ripped it away, and it was now loose. He began to run along the shore looking for it. Though certainly not in the predicament the poor people in "The Ledge" were, he was still in an awful bind. No one knew where he was, and with each passing moment he could envision himself stranded. In fact, his wife thought he had gone partridge hunting. Any search for him would have started upriver—not out toward the bay.

Night, and no one at all on the opposite shore. He might fire shots all night and no one would hear him. In fact, my farm is only a mile or so up a laneway from this lonely island, but at that time there might have been no one walking that shore for days.

Still, as luck would have it, he saw his canoe bobbing away from the land, with each outgoing wave, at the very tip of the island. He set his sights on it, figuratively speaking, and began to wade out into the swells, feeling the cold wind upon him. Each moment the canoe got farther, and the grey, seaweed-filled water got deeper. It was up to his knees, and then thighs, and then waist. He kept going, feeling the water lap higher up upon him, with his breath getting shorter because of the pressure of the water against his lungs.

The only thing that saved him: he was on the inside of the island, where the water is not as deep as on the far side. He had to hurry, knowing that he did not have an unlimited amount of time, and he managed, and he did just manage to get a fingertip on his canoe, when he was almost up to his chest in water. He proceeded to get a hand on the stern, and hold it, and finally kick it back to shore, where he picked up his rifle and his birds and made his way back to the mainland, shore, and home.

Sometimes deer will swim the river and out to that island. You might see deer signs there. Sheldrake Island is a place where, in the eighteenth and nineteenth centuries, they left sick and infested passengers from ships. Though it has a well and stakes of an old settlement, it is still wooded. (Since I wrote this a cottage has been built, and a family now summers there.)

Along the opposite shore, down from the road to my own property, large buck can be seen walking. I realize that all the animals we hunt are in a general proximity to water—either a brook or a river. I hunted them along the Fundy coast and saw them in the same hidden places. In fact I took them from those places long ago.

There are other islands that deer cross to. We have seen them on Beaubears Island upriver, and on many others. In the half summer light, fishing salmon, I saw a young mother doe and her fawn on the small, very small island beyond me up on the Norwest one night, grazing where low-growth alders and alder swale only hid them from view.

I wondered if she knew that made them both vulnerable. Perhaps it would have at another time, but this was midsummer and she was more concerned, or most concerned, about protecting her fawn, not from coyotes or man but from the mosquitoes and blackflies that will drive them crazy on summer nights. The wind off the water must have helped this a little.

Two years later, in the deep fall of the year, with just a presence of snow and the water cold on my waders, I made my way across to that island—again, with no one knowing where I was (irresponsible, I know, but many times we only get a real sense of where we must go when we start to go there).

The water was not deep but the rocks were all sizes, and slippery—though my waders were padded at the bottom, I am not the most sure person on my feet. I was carrying a backpack, and my rifle over my shoulder. I made it onto the island sometime after two in the afternoon and sat at the edge of a deer trail that led up from the water into some distant overgrowth and forlorn naked bushes. I sat there camouflaged and hunkered down, with buck musk masking my scent, until almost dark, with my feet freezing in those fishing waders. Suddenly I realized that retracing my way back across the river, while unable to see into it, was going to be a difficult thing for me, so I started back across with the twilight very red beneath the hilltop trees, and already the sound of coyotes yapping to each other along the ridge above. Halfway across that river, picking my way along, I look up to see a large—and I mean huge—buck simply watching me from the shore. He very well may have been on his way to that island—but here I was standing in the middle of the river. I had nowhere to put my backpack so I could sling my rifle around and raise it. Of course I attempted to do just that, and my backpack hit the water as I moved my rifle to my shoulder. The deer simply bounded away, tail in the air and a tree limb crashing. I turned and had to follow my backpack, up to my waist in water, and grabbed it—and made it across to the shore feeling as foolish as hell.

I remember years ago Mike Kenny, one of the finest woodsmen I have had the privilege to know, shot two deer on an island on the Sovogle River, sometime in the late afternoon, after tracking them down the hills from his camp for hours. He knew they must have crossed, so he waited on the shore, hoping to catch a sight of them. Finally his patience was rewarded, and he saw them appear, just before dark, and was able to shoot both. Then by himself he had to construct a bridge across that water, walk over, gut and clean the deer, and carry them back one at a time over the swift rapids where his bridge was laid. The buck was over two hundred pounds, the doe a hundred and fifty.

He finished doing this in the dark and made it back to camp that freezing night, sometime in the mid-1960s. These were just two of the many deer he would take up near his camp at Mile 6 of the Fraser Burchill Road. I hunted with him on one of those occasions, and realized this fellow could live in the woods by himself without any problem. These feats, accomplished by ordinary men I grew up beside, give credit to the people, as people who have retained their heritage because they take it seriously. A hunter the calibre of Mr. Kenny could tell a visitor from Ontario or New York about the world of New Brunswick a hundred times more significantly than the brochures at bed-and-breakfasts and historic King's Landing.

8

In the seventeen and eighteen hundreds in Europe, people could get lost on major roads. Lord Macaulay writes that, setting aside the alphabet and the printing press, "those inventions which abridge distance have done most for the civilization of our species." Road improvements were crucial in those days, as roads were difficult to distinguish and follow, and even Samuel Pepys and his wife lost their way more than once while travelling on a main road in their coach in England. This was also a common occurrence in France and the Netherlands.

In the early days of our camp beyond Mile 17 of Mullin Stream Road, there were times when, setting out on the deer trails in early morning, I would be turned about by eleven o'clock. It was then that I would have to remind myself that I was between roads and a major stream, and though I thought I was in a difficult predicament it was just my imagination. This always worked. It made a world of difference to realize that any direction I took was the right one, unless I went in complete figure eights or circles.

A friend of mine from Nova Scotia on a bird hunt with his dog was lost completely for hours in the middle of nowhere, one day outside of Amherst, because he had gone off the road to search for a wounded bird and had continued into a place he was less familiar with. Soon he found himself stumbling about, trying to backtrack, with no sense at all of what direction he had come, or what direction he was going. Looking up at the trees above his head only baffled him more. It was early in the season, the trees still had leaves, and the forest was dense. He had no idea after a while where to go. He finally decided, rightly, to sit where he was, and wait—at least until he calmed down. It was his dog that helped him find his way out, by running up to him, running away until he disappeared, and running back to him again. My friend realized that the dog was showing him the way back home.

It was a long day, but he did make it back.

When I brought Jeb Stuart, my little river water dog, with me on fishing journeys back in the late 1980s and early 1990s, there was never any worry about being lost, for all I had to do, no matter where I was, was say "Truck," and Jeb would simply turn and start back to it, stopping at intervals to wait for me.

People can bring matches and be dressed warmly and comfortably, but if they panic it doesn't matter, even if the highway is three hundred yards away. I heard the story of a man years ago leaving a lake and taking the one direction that was wrong. That is, any other direction would have led him to civilization in a matter of an hour. But having lost the path, and after walking around the entire circumference of the lake two or three times trying to find it, he started through the woods in the one direction that took him farther and farther into the wilderness. He was lost for three days, and when they finally found him he was walking a road twenty miles from where the search party was, most of his clothes torn off. But he was alive.

Many of the people who don't live are children who get lost in the summer, down in a bog or cedar swamp, where they are far from earshot of their parents' cries. Whole weeks are devoted to trying to find these children, and many are never found, or when they are they have already succumbed to thirst and terror. Since my boys live close to the woods in the summer I am as conscious of this as other fathers and worry about it as much. And though I am also conscious that as a child I roamed the woods with friends day in and day out, without concern, it is natural to worry. Yet all the worrying in the world doesn't help. I remember, years back, going with a woman to check a farmhouse she wanted to buy. My oldest boy, who was four at the time, jumped from the car and, without knowing it, ran two feet by an open well that would have dropped him eighty feet in a second. None of us knew the well was there. How many nightmares I have had because I didn't prevent him from running by what I wasn't aware of, and yet how little I could have done!

There are documented cases of children lost who say the fairies found and took care of them. One, a child lost for nine or ten days and given up for dead, said the fairies brought her food and helped keep her warm. I suppose everyone would take this as completely delusional, except for her parents.

The most sensible suggestion to those who are mixed up in the woods is to stay put. This is the easiest advice to give and yet the hardest to follow, for a variety of reasons. Movement seems like action, action seems like advancement. So if I move I am helping myself advance. This is almost never the case if you are seriously lost. But so many people are determined, and panicked, and wish to find their way out as soon as possible. The heart rate goes up, the thinking gets blurred, and soon one is more lost than before.

"They will find you" is actually true more often if you stay where you are. But it is easy to say and hard to do. The fact that you have to admit defeat and actually stay where the hell you are is hard to take. I'm playing the pragmatist here. I know what it is like to keep going when you feel you are lost, because I have done it, and have been lucky enough to stumble upon a road. I have also been turned around with others, who have known the woods better than I, and have taken heart in the fact that they did know. Though on occasion they too were as confused about direction as I was. Once, on a fishing trip with Peter McGrath, we were seriously mixed up, and finally had to rely on something neither of us believed was accurate: a compass.

When I took my father's car on those partridge outings years ago I couldn't let him know where I was going because I was doing something he didn't want me to do. But I did have the car. Other times I have found myself hunting deer and realizing late in the day that I have told no one I was doing this. Once I had a deer down and had to haul it half a mile. No one knew where I was. My wife Peg was at work in a city 104 miles away. She knew I was gone hunting on the Miramichi. My father, still alive at that time, had no idea where I was.

That is foolish. But many people have no idea of their plans.

One year, Peter McGrath was hunting up off the hardwood ridges along the Plaster Rock Highway. He had been advised by friends to take a compass with him, for the ridges looked dangerously alike, and he might find himself on a ridge far from the ridge he believed he was on. These ridges intersect one another at all angles and can leave the hunter confused within a half hour of walking into them. The hardwood birches and poplar trees go on for miles, so at times the land looks identical, and if you are not careful you can become seriously lost. But Peter was young then, and brash. He had walked rivers all day long, cut through as much woods as most woodsmen. He had hunted and fished alone far from civilization, and he believed in his own wits, and in no one else's.

"I started out fine," he told me. "I came to a small brook running between two hardwood ridges and I followed it up a ways, and picked up a deer trail. I knew where the brook was, and therefore where I had left my truck, and was certain that I could follow this buck, no problem." And that is what he did. He followed the buck until late in the day. He saw it, crossing the top of a ridge far ahead of him. He raised his rifle but couldn't take the shot, and he knew it was getting late, and he would not have a chance at it again that afternoon. Still, he wanted to go to the top of that faraway ridge to see if he might spy it again.

When he got there, somewhat winded, he saw the tracks of another hunter. But, to his surprise and consternation,

he realized that these were his own tracks. That is, somewhere along his route he had travelled in a complete
circle—and, what was more alarming, probably not once
but twice. And in that case he wasn't sure where to pick
this circle up. He began following those tracks backwards,
but felt that these would only take him to where he had
spied that deer going over the ridge. And sure enough that
is what happened. Now he was very confused, for his own
tracks only took him in a circle—which meant he had
crossed himself up on some ridge and had no way to determine where his truck was.

He began to look through his field glasses to see if he
could notice anything promisingly familiar, but unfortunately the strong birch trees stretched away up and down
various ridges and at many angles. The day was growing
later and the sun was fainting away among the hills of trees
and snow. He started back to the ridge he believed the
brook must run through. But when he got there it looked
terribly unfamiliar, and there wasn't a sign of his tracks or
his buck's tracks. But there were the tracks of a smaller
buck. He realized he had to stay put for the night if he
didn't find his way back soon. Besides, everything looked
the same. And he decided that his friends were right, he
should have brought a compass. But then, just as twilight
was coming, he decided he would follow those small buck
tracks just to see where they went. As he did, he crossed
between two ridges, and he noticed that this smaller buck
had gone down to the one thing Peter was familiar with—
the brook. Once at the brook he followed it down two
hundred yards and came first to the big buck tracks he had
spied that morning, and then to the tracks he had made

when he'd first entered. He followed these for ten minutes and he was back at his truck, just as it was getting dark.

I arrived at our camp on Mullin Stream Road on a cold November afternoon over twenty years ago now. I had come in to see my brother, who had gone hunting with a friend of his earlier that day. I got to the camp at about four o'clock and stoked the stove. I started to boil some water for a salmon I'd brought, which I had taken in late July from the south branch of the Sovogle at the Three Minute Pool, and I waited for them to return. It was after five, and dark, and still no sign of them. Cold rain, mixed with snow, started to fall out of a black sky. The night was soundless, and all the old spruce growth was grey as ash.

John's half-ton was parked at the camp, so I knew they were on foot. And I thought there were only two or three places they would likely be. One was across the Mullin Stream, about a mile away, where my brother-in-law had just jumped a huge buck a few days before. Another was in toward the falls, where there was always a sign of deer. And the third was near Davy's Lake. I waited, thinking that they would be along soon. They weren't. Finally I took the water off the stove, took my jeep, and went out to Mile 17, where I sounded the horn.

No response. It was now well after six o'clock. It was silent, and the rain had turned to snow. I drove the jeep up the side road, onto an old overgrown logging road that had not been used in thirty years or more. There I parked and, taking a flashlight, walked into the woods, along a deer trail that brought me out at the small hidden lake I hunted so much, that I had taken two deer from, but never the deer I wanted, the buck I believed was in there.

I could see that they had been there, earlier—or at least someone had. But when I got to the lake, everything was silent and black. The trees there are black spruce, very close together. It is hard to see game, and you have to be silent and wait for the animals moving down their small trails to come to you. It would be very easy to lose an eye there, in the dark.

I called—no answer. Finally I raised my rifle to the air and fired a shot. I waited. Far away, on the far side of the lake, a shot was fired from John's twelve-gauge shotgun. I turned and went back to the jeep, drove out to 17 Mile Road again, and fired another.

I was answered. They were about half a mile into the woods, between the lake and the road. Not so bad, except it was pitch-black and they probably had no real sense of direction. I followed the sound, halfway up the road, and, turning the small jeep on the road, pointed my lights directly into the woods and fired again, into the air. Soon I could hear them, and I answered back, and by my answers they made it out.

How had this happened—to be on the far side of that hidden lake?

Late in the day, just as they were about to leave, they'd seen a buck on the far side. They'd tried to get closer to it, and of course found themselves at dark in an unfamiliar area. As the day darkened, all the trees became as ghostly as ash, silent and muted. The fellow with John became more and more hysterical as the day darkened. He kept falling to his knees and crawling about.

"Look for stumps," he kept yelling at John. "Look for stumps."

"Now why would I look for stumps?" John said.

"It means humanity," the fellow kept saying. "It means humanity—it means we are close to humanity."

"Buddy, we're only half a mile up the road from two camps," John said.

They found stumps, stumps cut up on that old logging road, maybe thirty or forty years ago, by men long gone and ghosts. They hadn't a match between them. And no one knew where they were.

"Humanity or no, unless we hear a car, so we can figure out direction, we're here for the night," John said. "We'll find our way back to the lake in the morning."

"We can keep going," the fellow said.

"Keep going, one of us will lose an eye," John answered.

It would have been a damn cold night. But I happened to take a run back to see him and fired that shot into the air. Even though they had an idea of where they were, they were in no real position to keep bulling themselves out of the woods.

Once, a fellow I was supposed to meet at Portage River didn't show up until almost two hours later. I waited as the day got black and the coyotes began yelping and rounding each other up. We were on an upland road, and each of us had taken a different direction. I had, as usual, hunted in a small back field surrounded by swale, waiting on deer that would move back and forth. But I hadn't seen a deer that day. My friend was a hunter who had to keep on the move.

I fired a shot and honked my horn, and waited. Finally he came out of the woods, where he had collected a friend's traps, and told me I shouldn't have worried about him, and gave me one of his large rakings about it. But I believe to this day he had gotten turned about, and my honking the horn helped him. Though I cannot say, nor would he.

Some people don't mind being a little lost, because they have enough experience and faith in themselves to match the difficulty. The great opponent, the imagination, is kept in check. No one has written more profoundly about how imagined terrors can direct your life than Joseph Conrad in *Lord Jim*. A young officer on a merchant ship panics, thinking the ship is about to sink, and deserts his post with the rest of the crew, leaving two hundred passengers to die. They decide on a story in which they valiantly tried to save them, only to find that not only did the ship not sink, but it was towed to port before their lifeboat got there.

The imagination causes panic when no panic is necessary. This is the worst enemy in the wilderness, or anywhere else. Years ago my friend David Savage used to hunt deer on the birch ridges along the Restigouche. He always got deer there—he was and is a fine tracker. But tracking an animal can cause problems. Now and again he knew he was lost, but he always managed to find his car. Getting lost on birch ridges is extremely easy. One ridge looks very much like the other. Unfortunately they trail off in very different directions, and if you are not careful you can be literally miles from where you think you are.

David explained to me that he never took a compass in those days, relying instead on his own intuition, which was always good. Sometimes he would have to backtrack two to three miles, and not find his car until well after dark. Oftentimes he told the friend he was with that he might be late, but he would return. Sometimes his friend, almost giving him up, would see him coming along two hours or more after dark.

It is, I suppose, like Daniel Boone's answer to the question about being lost.

"No, I was never lost," Boone asserted. "Though I was well mixed up for a month or two."

To David it was not a case of panic as much as an intellectual dilemma. He wondered why he was getting turned around at a certain spot, when he was sure he knew the area well. He determined to discover what his mistake was.

And he did. One late afternoon, he came on a friend of his tracking a deer that he himself was tracking and realized that he was over half a mile from where he'd thought he was, because he was on a completely different ridge. It was a slight misstep at the base where two ridges joined a third and crossed each other, but this misstep caused him to be turned around. Once he realized this, he was never turned about on those ridges again.

9

The night I went back to the Mullin Stream camp and brought John and his friend the fish, it started to snow. The woods here are thick and old, and it was ten years before the new road was pushed through by new logging considerations. So it was the old land of our ancestors still, people who had worked these roads and streams for lumber barons from the old days, and took moose and caribou for the lumbermen, and cut with axe and saw, and hauled wood by horse and two-sled. All of that age was an age ago the night I visited my brother, which seems to me an age ago now. The men who lived so much in hope and hardship were gone, ghosts from another era.

Soundlessly the snow fell through the old-growth forest, and we ate our dinner and played some cards. The boys had a beer or two, and John decided to stay up another day, to cross the old Mullin Stream bridge and make his way up along the tractor road at dawn. He did not much like hunting in where I hunted.

Hunting by the lake is a very different proposition to hunting in a chop-down or along a road, or in a stand, for that matter. Hunting in and about that old forgotten lake is my kind of hunting. A hunting done on the ground, near a deer mark or trail, and without sound, or movement. It is close, face-to-face hunting. There is a chance you will see nothing, and hear a deer as it passes by. It means that I have stood up to four or five hours in one spot completely silent and still, trying to keep my scope from fogging up. There are days I have done this from dawn to dusk and have seen nothing. On other days, however, deer walk through the growth and come almost up to me. And a big buck up close in swale, in rut, and close to two hundred pounds, is not guaranteed to be passive.

Even so, if I cannot see them I never risk a shot. (And now that the deer hunt is bucks only, it is absolutely essential you be absolutely sure it is a buck.) Or moose pass by unconcerned, now that moose season is over, or a bear crosses the river beneath me and saunters by, groggy with sleep.

John was up early, before light, and couldn't rouse his friend. Nor did he rouse me, since I had no intention of hunting. He poked about for some coffee, and made his way out before dawn. The light was just coming into the sky when he got to Mullin Stream. There he had to cross the icy pilings of a bridge torn down the year before, and he made his way up along the silent road, deserted and snow-covered, where thrashed-up and disposed trees lay on either side, a whole canopy of our woods on the ground. The snow had stopped, and everything was white and silent. Heavy snow hung off the muted branches of oak and birch; Mullin Stream had frozen and twisted away into the blurred corners of his vision, under a foot of snow. All was fresh, and there was hardly a stir of wind. This road twisted for a mile or two into the backwoods beyond Mullin Stream, where it came to a sudden, inexplicable stop, as if the men building it had decided they had not intended to go in that direction.

Soon John was up beyond the first bend, and the day was brightening. John hunts like my uncle, who hunted successfully with a twelve-gauge shotgun for years. He had a slug in the chamber, and number 7 birdshot in his pocket, for he was not interested in partridge this day. He looked down at the side of the logging road and saw a buck track, and then another, deep prints rounded off at the toes. It was a large deer, he knew.

At first he wasn't that excited, thinking the buck might have passed sometime in the night. But there would have been a topping of snow on the hoofprint if that had been the case—and the print was bare, with some slight bluish compressed water at the base. And the buck had not crossed the road, but had turned and was walking ahead of him, somewhere up beyond the next turn. When he realized this, he paid much more attention. Judging by the length between the tracks, the deer was not in a hurry, it was moving leisurely up the centre of the road. The fluffy light snow had made John's walk almost soundless. John took the safety off and moved carefully to the right side, as if walking on eggshells. Then he looked ahead—and sure enough the deer was standing broadside, looking back at him.

It might have been well over a hundred yards, and he had a shotgun, not a rifle. That is, he had no real sights. You point a shotgun, and anything over a hundred yards can be unpredictable. Still, it was a shot he had to take, knowing that if he moved the deer would bolt. He had to bring the shotgun up and fire in one quick motion, and that is what he did. He raised the shotgun just shoulder high, pointed, and fired, as the buck was beginning to jump. The buck hit the shoulder of the road and disappeared. John put another slug in the chamber and walked quickly ahead.

Back at our cabin, John's friend was awake, and called over to me.

"I heard a shotgun."

This piqued my interest.

"Birdshot, maybe."

"No, it was a slug, I'm sure."

He might have been firing at a partridge and forgot he had a slug in, I thought—that happens on occasion. Or it very well could have been someone else; the shot was far enough away. But I was up, and we were both out the door.

We headed along the camp road, to Mile 17, where we heard a second shot. We waited a moment, but there was no more. We crossed the bridge, covered in ice, and ran up the other side as fast as we could. And we followed John's tracks up the silent road and into the woods. Where John fired the first shot, we saw the spent shell. There John's tracks moved quicker. Where the buck had jumped, there were spots of blood. Across the ditch was the second shell.

The buck was down, just off the road. It had fallen in a small clearing. The first shot had hit it in the neck, on the run, so it was a fine shot. The second shot had been to kill the wounded animal.

It was an eight-point buck—but very heavy, and the tines were thick and broad. We helped John get it out. He had, by chance, forgotten his knife, and I, by chance, had brought mine. You never need a large knife to dress an animal down. The huge knives they have in those stores are ridiculous. In fact, when I was younger a man came into the woods with us all the time wearing a knife with a ten-inch blade, two bullet belts strapped across his chest, and camouflage grease for his face. He was a good enough lad, walked stealthily, etc., but I guarantee you he never once shot a deer. Often he would pull out his huge knife, look at his reflection in its gleam, sharpen it with a stone, then look over at me and smile.

I've seen David Savage take the hide off a moose with a small three-and-a-half or four-inch blade. Anything else is not needed, and might damage the carcass.

After we dressed the animal we carried it back across Mullin Stream, put it on the truck, and were out by mid-morning, the thought of John's experience the night before, in the black spruce, long put behind him. It is a strange part of fate but I missed a deer almost the same way the year before, up on a road near the Norwest at the end of deer season. I was coming out at dusk, and walked right up behind a buck, which stopped and turned to watch me. I made the mistake of taking a step as I took the safety off, and with one bound the great tail came up, and the deer was gone, into the healthy gloom of a cold November night.

There are, of course, other ways to be lost.

10

I have eaten porcupine and beaver, frog and groundhog—all for the sake of expedience, and as a kind of formal declaration that these things can be used if a man in the woods is in difficulty. I am sure all of these things were eaten by many in bygone days, by the Micmac and Maliseet, by ancestors of mine. The Micmac were and are hunters and hunted caribou and moose for generations, and I have been told that their diet consisted mainly of meat, fish, and berries picked by the women. They captured beaver in their winter dens and were able to run moose to the ground. I doubt if much was wasted by them, of bear or fish or fowl. They were the first and ablest guides of the great era of non-resident game hunting, when men from other nations found us a wilderness place to be, to hunt or fish. Of course, foods like frog are still a delicacy.

I thought of all of this one night when I was on a plane, going down to Windsor, Ontario, to give a reading. I was at the back of the plane and the weather was wild; there was a chop the plane was against the entire way. It was a prop plane, and we were squeezed together. There, on the other side, just down from my seat, were five American hunters, travelling home from a successful hunt. I thought a hunt in northern Ontario, but as they spoke I realized it was a trip into northern Saskatchewan. They were buoyant and uncomplicated in their glee. All except one, maybe, had lucked in and had taken deer. I am not sure, but I assumed it was mule deer, although it very well may have been white-tail. Both deer are there, I think. I do not know the land of northern Saskatchewan, and I am sure I never will, and I am no less certain that I will never need to. I have enough land of my own.

I was sure by the way they spoke that they were from the northern States, and most likely hunted there, so, it meant that they were on a big deer hunt—which is not hyperbole, but the hunt for large buck deer. So they had made reservations, and had travelled by plane, with their rifles, to a hunting lodge in the North. But there was an unfortunate side to this hunt. I do not mention this with the intention of it reflecting poorly on all American hunters. Most are wonderful people all the way around. But these five were very festive in their amusement about the backward people of Saskatchewan, and how little they knew about hunting. As they spoke, I realized a few things. The people they were amused by—those who "shot a deer and it didn't matter the size"—were the very people who had taken care of them in this wilderness setting. And I would make a bet that none of them would have lucked in to anything without the very people their cynicism now emasculated. And that these people "who drove cars with bald tires," as one reminisced over his bourbon, were men who in any way and in any day would have outlasted these men in the woods, and walked them into the ground in a second. (I guarantee I would have.)

If those they ridiculed shot deer without trophy racks, it was because they used their game for something these men might never have needed to—they used the deer for food, not trophies. I realized that so much of the animosity toward people like this comes not because they are manly killers, but because they are boyishly naïve. They are, in the main, what urban ideas have done to the hunt. Animals are no longer animals to certain hunters. They are trophies. They are not used for food—they are used for show. They hunt for big racks, and are guided to big racks by someone whose own relatives may shoot a spike horn, or a non-trophy buck, knowing the quality of the meat will be better—or they might even realize that too many big bucks taken changes the genetics of the very animal. This is at least as important as bragging rights over a fourteen-point buck.

None of these men had shot a fourteen-point buck, and I did not lean over and tell them that I had. What I did do, however, was defend these certain fellows from Saskatchewan whom I did not know, had never met, and who might not ever defend me. I did say that these men didn't hunt for trophies—it was a different hunt altogether, and one that was just as noble. In fact, I bet them that these men might have been the very ones who built the insulated tree stands that those hunters sat in comfortably to shoot huge buck without knowing much about the land, the people, or the animals at all. That perhaps these fellows had placed those stands exactly where they would offer the best opportunity for a rack that any half-assed shots could take home, with bragging rights, to their wives.

They stared at me in that self-complicated silence that unknowing people often have, their brows screwed up, and, as always happens with me, sooner or later I cursed myself for my tongue. One of the youngsters was perhaps nineteen, and he believed his taking a deer made him brave—and who was I, this middle-aged man who almost never went out on a hunt any more, to try to dash a self-delusion that all of us should have for a while in our youth? I didn't want to dash it so much as tell them that they hadn't really been on a hunt, that perhaps none of them would have made out as well in those woods on their own as the men they now, in comfort, mocked. That, in fact, was the essential point—they had always been in comfort. The whole point of hunting lodges, from what I knew about them, from the midpoint of the nineteenth century on, was to keep hunters in relative comfort, to feed them, to amuse them if need be, to guide them to the animals they were to kill. My uncles were guides who did this half a century ago, and my cousins and friends were guides who did this now. And how in God's name could they say anything about anyone with "bald tires" who took a deer to feed his family? In fact, the very point of hunting was that which they now in ignorance defamed, and which the urban world that looked upon nature as "pretty" did not understand.

So much of it was amusing to them. Would it have been amusing to them if I had told them that the Micmac captured beaver from their dens by first patting them? Would they have ever been able to do the same?

These were the hunters so many who don't hunt see.

And I realized that hunting, or the terrible reputation it has among "civilized" men and women, is and can be its own worst enemy. And one reason for this is that hunting is now a product of that very civilization that decries discomfort and work, and ingenuity, and in the end bravery. In relative terms, so much care is taken of those hunters who pay big bucks for their hunt that they might just as well be at a health spa for the weekend. Some of the hunting done is on the same level as travelling middle-class retirees visiting a bed-and-breakfast near Annapolis Royal. I know a good fellow who never shot a deer, and tried each year to. He was fed up with his inability—once, standing on a rut mark, a deer walked right past him, and he didn't see it until it was beyond his range. Finally he paid for his deer by going to one of these lodges. He knew he had, and it did not sit well with him, and in the end he was teased as much about this as he had ever been teased for not getting a deer. I prefer not to tease him. I know we all have our own inconstancy; our own grand design is not really our own but given to us by some Higher Power we do not understand.

There is much rancour about this kind of killing. But I am not faulting those who make a living by it. They still set up a hunt that is essentially industrious and workable. In the old days, and perhaps still, they hired Indian guides. In fact, at the first of the last century most of the guides for men like Braithwaite et al. were Micmac or Maliseet, and without a doubt they were the finest guides in the province. In a way, the terms of the hunt have not changed at all. Men are relied upon to take other men to the game. There is nothing wrong with this, but one should know which side of the square root of the equation he is on, and be mindful and humble about this. Writers, themselves, some who are terrified of guns, have made a great deal over this—and writers who have never been in the wilderness speak with authority about the First Nations. I am all right with this, except it is an obsession among Canadian writers to demonstrate how well they know the soul of the First Nations people. In some ways it is understandable. Though, in the end, it never does justice to the Micmac, Huron, Cree, or Sioux.

These boyish hunters flying with me to Windsor, laughing at the men from Saskatchewan, are the personification of this debate. The only thing I believed was that I would not hunt with these fellows claiming their racks, and that their guides in northern Saskatchewan perhaps did not respect them. I wondered how many of them, set down in a woods, would last. Not as many, I didn't think, as those they bullied with their comments. In the movie *The Deer Hunter*, the character played by Robert De Niro hunts a big buck along mountain ravines with one bullet in the chamber, while his friend kills a little doe in the small pond outside the cabin by firing nine shots into it. My contention is that many of the fellows travelling on that plane resembled not the former character but the latter, and there was no way to make them see it.

11

In the 1930s my wife's grandfather hunted both deer and bear on the Bartibog, and guided as well. Many nights my wife's family relied upon game to eat. In my earliest days I heard of mighty bear in the Bartibog region. In the early years there was a bounty on the animals, looked upon as a nuisance. They were trapped and shot whenever people had a chance. Now, living on the Bartibog four or five months of the year, I see bear regularly in the spring. Deer come into our fields all summer long. Does and fawns stand in my garden.

My dog no longer chases those deer—at fourteen years old and with bad hips, she runs out to the shed and barks. When I yell to her to sit, she lies on her belly and watches the deer graze. She knows that she no longer has a chance at catching them. Or maybe she has gained wisdom over the years and now leaves them be.

Wayne Curtis has gained as much wisdom as anyone. In the early years he hunted with his father, and depended upon it. He remembers, when he was a boy, his father shooting moose for the winter. One was shot with an old Boer War rifle at well over three hundred yards. He also remembers his father as a guide being accidentally shot in the arm, by another guide, along the Cains River in the early 1950s. I imagine they were guiding for a deer hunt. Many thought he would lose the arm, and for days they didn't know if he would be able to function on the farm any more.

To Wayne, knowing the things of the wilderness, of the deep woods, was something people of his generation were taught to believe was instrumental. Years before this accident, Wayne's grandfather was on perhaps the last caribou hunt in New Brunswick. Fish and deer and other wildlife were as much a part of their diet as hamburger and fries might be for the kids today.

He hunted birds as a boy with a slingshot, and later on, deer with a rifle. He was an excellent shot with both. I have seen him walk along the roadways trying to find smooth stones to carry. He took many deer from the woods, and hunted every year. Even now, though he no longer hunts deer, he carries a slingshot with him along the old trails that meander near the main Souwest River, where he has his guiding camp (he has forty years' experience as a guide, and has guided me to fish on more than one occasion), and he searches for birds in the popal or birch trees on late-fall afternoons. These are the best times to hunt for birds, just at dusk when the wind has died down and night is coming on. The birds rise to the trees and sit above the ground. You have to be careful, and stalk them, as you would any game, and, using a slingshot, you have to be able to get almost under them to fire.

Those trails and overgrown fields bring him back to a time that was simpler and, in many respects, kinder. To hit a bird with a slingshot and bring it down—which he did once on the fly—is great sportsmanship.

He was a hunter from the time he was a boy—and essentially it was what saved him, when he came back from the industrial cities of Ontario where he had gone to work. In those cities, and from his exceptional writing, you begin to get a glimpse of what it was like to be a Maritimer in the 1950s and '60s. We were left out of the equation, as certain of our third-class citizenship as any people of the day. Wayne didn't have it easy. He was self-taught, did not finish high school, yet his strength of character and his writing ability earned him a large audience, much respect, and an honorary doctorate. As a young man trying to earn a living and help support his family by sending home money, he also learned to play golf as well as some men who had much more privilege and opportunity.

When he finally came back from those industrial cities, realizing that, as a Maritimer, those cities would never belong to him, he would go every day into the woods, with his rifle and knapsack. He said his main object was not to kill, but to simply do something that was so much a part of the natural world, after being so long immersed in the urban one. The short, cold autumn afternoons, with the sky filled with snow clouds and the world folding into itself for winter, made his spirit soar. He had to once again connect with who he was. He would take a few provisions, and carry his Winchester lever-action, and follow deer trails along rushing half-frozen brooks. Sometimes he would follow a deer for miles, through the dense spruce hills, and catching sight of it decide not to fire. Up along the Cains River, he was able to be alone, with the scent of autumn on the foliage. There, he said, he gave up deer almost every other day, and said to himself: "No, that's not the one." That is, he was like many hunters—more compassionate than they are sometimes given credit for.

In fact, Wayne Curtis's story about giving up deer doesn't surprise me. I know many, many hunters who have done this. It was to him the least significant part of hunting. Like Jason, his son, who is a guide to bird hunters from the States, it is the quest that is important. The fact of being ethical is a stamp of honour.

One time, Wayne followed a deer for miles along the hills above a frozen river. It trailed away into the gloom of early dusk. There was a heavy snow in the woods, and Wayne had been waiting on snow to track. But the snow was deeper than usual at that time of year. Wayne's hands were frozen raw on his weapon. The deer knew it was being followed, and tried to lose him. It was a big deer, with a ten-point rack. Wayne got to see it twice that day, and did not get it in his sights. He had seen this deer on many occasions before as well, but had not been able to track it successfully. This day, however, he was determined—determined to prove to himself that he had not lost himself in the mire of Ontario's industry. He began to track this deer in early morning, and this went on for some hours, and sometimes Wayne was up to his knees in snow, and had to navigate hillsides slippery with frost and ice. When he caught up to it, late in the afternoon, the deer was exhausted and had stumbled on icy shore boulders, and was an easy shot.

Wayne, only about fifty yards away when he stepped out on the shore, raised his rifle and took the safety off. But didn't take the shot.

"No, that's not the one," he said, putting the rifle down, and he smiled to himself. All that way, all those miles of woods, he had been able to do what one man in five hundred might—he had been able, like men of the old days, to track a deer to ground.

It is important to know that this is a feat, tracking deer down, that very few hunters ever get to accomplish. A feat that those in the union halls of Ontario who made sport of him and his "Newfie" accent might never match. For many hunters today, going into the woods alone is something they have no stomach for. They have been given the "things" that render them dependent on the world, and even hunting doesn't take them away from this dependence. They ride in comfortable truck cabs and look out over chop-downs from which wood and trees have been pulled to be sent to other nations. There might be deer there, hides almost orange in the sun, and they can take the shot. But to track a deer for miles, or to refuse to leave the hunt because an animal is injured, is the domain of the best hunter.

Tracking deer requires a kind of stamina and intelligence that many hunters don't possess, or don't have time to learn. If you leave an office on Friday afternoon to drive to your camp, and stay up Saturday, and hunt in and about the camp roads—this is fine, and it is the way that many of us hunt. (I hunt this way now.) But it is not conducive to being a good hunter.

A good hunter goes where the deer tracks take him or her. You have to be as silent and careful as possible, and your sense of direction has to be impeccable, especially along the hardwood ridges up along the Saint John River, because in a matter of moments you might find yourself in deep woods. Just like the gentleman David Savage was hunting with up on the Restigouche, not everyone has this ability. The deer I have shot when tracking have been few, and I have been lucky—once because I lost the tracks and had turned to go when the buck came up behind me. I don't call that a success—just luck. My hunt is called still hunting—that is, I cross into deer territory, find where the buck has scraped, and wait. Wait, and wait.

Wayne knew how to track them, and didn't shoot.

He shot his last deer some years ago in the field behind his home. He never felt right about taking that deer, for the deer had been there all summer.

I have seen him intentionally lose fish, realizing that he has had many in his day. (I have seen David Savage do this as well.)

Wayne has all of this as a lament now. He is a plain-spoken, good-hearted man who has lived his life as close to the woods as anybody I know. But the woods have gone, or at least are changed forever. The camp where he once guided fishermen has been taken over by hunters from Alabama. And though I have liked most of the people from Alabama I have met, there is something disconcerting about this.

The world no longer belongs to us. In so many ways, we are now in the same position the First Nations peoples found themselves in. Thinking this, and multiplying it a thousand times, we might begin to realize the tragedy that occurred here four hundred years ago.

There were no snowmobiles or four-wheelers, or many four-wheel drive trucks when Wayne was a boy. The trails weren't as broad or as well marked as they are today. This is what allowed him to learn how to hunt on foot and on his own.

One day, in deep wood, with snow on the boughs of spruce, far up along the main Souwest Miramichi River, Jason Curtis shot a deer that had come over a hill into view. It was a long shot in dense wood, but he knew he had wounded it, and he began to track, for he would never leave a wounded animal. He tracked it for three hours, down through swampy and marshy ground. He was on its trail but he couldn't seem to catch it. Then the buck seemed to make a conscious decision to go up against the current when he came to a brook. And Jason had to trust his instinct that this was where the deer had travelled, even though all his experience told him the deer would travel down current. So he turned up along the slippery brook in the cold, splendid autumn day. He kept looking at the leaves floating down in the current. By this he surmised how fast the deer was moving. Then, just when he thought he'd been mistaken and was about to turn back, he saw something on one of those leaves that floated past him. It was a spot of blood. He kept moving. Soon he saw more, on some stone. And finally he was able to find the eight-point buck on the shore, far upriver.

He had a long haul with an animal well over two hundred pounds, but he dressed it out, and made it back to camp by nightfall.

12

Years ago, David Savage began to hunt along the stretches of the Bartibog River, in Northumberland County, New Brunswick. He was an average kid of that time. He was a fine hockey player and a good baseball player. He was a fair student. But more than anything else, like so many boys here, he was an avid fisherman and hunter. He would listen to the tales told by his father, who was a fisheries officer, and uncles around the wood stove on cold winter nights, tales about the woods, and its trails, its uncompromising grace, and the animals hunted. The difference between a buck track and a doe track, or the difference between a cow call and a bull, or a bull track and a cow, if it was a young bull. How to react when a bull charges, how to call one almost to you. The way to track deer—how a deer sometimes tries to move behind you, in order to watch you. How to let a wounded animal, especially a moose or bear, go and lie down before you begin to track it.

The main thing these stories gave him was a desire to hunt as well. And by the time he was sixteen he was hunting on his own. He would leave school each autumn afternoon and, taking his 30-30, go into the woods. Waiting on a trail filled with the scent of autumn, of musk and bark and fallen leaves, he would listen for deer that moved out toward the back fields at twilight. His was not an idyllic childhood, far from it—but it was an exceptionally fortunate one in certain respects. Along those back autumn fields downriver was a good place to learn to hunt. There, in the late gloom of one long-ago afternoon, he shot his first deer, a spike horn, about 130 pounds, as it moved along the pine and spruce in back of a field. He hunted birds, as well, those grey-feathered partridge with their glossy necks and beautiful heads. He hunted them with a shotgun or .22 rifle, and became a good shot, and had an excellent eye for spotting game. In fact, most of the men I write about in these pages have an uncanny ability to spot game, either deer or moose or bird, where 80 percent of humans might pass them by, not noticing. He went on duck hunts, and learned how to call ducks and geese that flew in the large sky over Bartibog Island.

The second year he went deer hunting he shot an eight-point buck, and after that, time after time he spent the deer season away from most people, by himself in the woods, either on the Miramichi or along the Restigouche, with an old army sack filled with a lunch, an extra bullet or two, and a skinning knife. In fact, the first time I heard of David, my wife, who is his cousin, described him as a fisherman and a hunter. He was eighteen at the time. And he has gained a great deal of wisdom since then.

Sometimes he hunted deer with buckshot, and he carried number 6 birdshot that he could change to very quickly when he needed it.

Soon even the back trails were too crowded for him, and he meandered his way deeper into the woods, to hunt alone. He realized that when fly fishing the hard-running small rivers on the Miramichi, or the vast pools of the Restigouche, one would often meet people, and hunting was the one activity for which there was still enough comfortable woods that he could be entirely by himself. Besides, he could prove to himself that he knew the woods as well as most, and prove that to others by being there. So complete was his comfort that he would tell those he was with never to worry about him if he was not back at dark, for he would find his way, sooner or later—and his hunt was such that he often waited in a spot until almost the last light, before he took the clip out of his rifle and headed back, making his way out to his car on those long autumn nights, walking miles in complete darkness. I can attest to this from the days when I hunted with him.

"Just because hunters haven't seen deer does not mean there aren't deer," he told me. "Most of the men hunting pick a road near woods, and wait—or a side logging road is the farthest into the woods they go. That is fine—for them—and there will be deer crossing those roads to and from their scrapes. The best thing, however, is to go beyond or behind those places, mooch about in the real wild, in where the deer live."

One day, leaving the small 2.2 Mile Road that years ago ran above the south branch of the Sovogle (with all the new chop-downs and work this road might very well be a memory now), and leaving hunters who had posted themselves on that road to catch deer crossing in the very early morning, David walked down toward the water just after daylight—and a half mile below that road, where the hunters waited, he heard a deer approaching. It was just light in the woods. The deer had crossed the river at 2.2 Mile Pool far below and was making its way up toward its rut marks on the high ground at daylight. It would travel in this pattern, coming back to all its rut marks over a three-day period. Now David heard it on the lower ground as it made its way toward him. He took the safety off and waited. Soon the buck came up over the embankment, almost in front of him, and he felled it with one shot—a 280-pound buck that the men above him were still waiting for. It took him well over an hour to dress and drag it back up the long-overgrown hill toward where those men, confident they were hunting a wilderness road, waited. The men were amazed to see the large buck he had taken.

And that was not the largest buck he ever shot. The largest buck weighed over 305 pounds, which is a monster buck. He tells the story, which I am sure is true, of being offered any amount of money to give up the tines of this great buck, by an American hunter in a truck stop one autumn day. He of course refused, but he never hunted for the tines. He never was a trophy hunter. Still, he took an eighteen-point non-typical buck (with a rack that wasn't completely symmetrical) one year when I was living in Saint John, and drove into the yard with it. It was the only year I shot a doe, if I remember correctly, just before doe season ended. (I never felt good about it, and I mention it because I never felt good about it.)

I have never seen a larger rack on a deer, although I am sure they exist. But this was a mythical deer. The year before that, he had shot a twelve-point buck on a dead run across a field in South Napan by leading it just a little, and knowing exactly when to fire. You don't practise a shot like that, you either have it in your arsenal or you don't. But David is an excellent shot with any kind of rifle, and, like Wayne Curtis, is an expert fisherman and guide, without being written up in any guidebook.

One of the things growing up along the river gave David was a love of canoes, and he is an expert in a canoe. The canoe he has used most often on the Miramichi and its tributaries is one called a Norwester, made by Ralph Mullin. It is a sturdy and wonderfully responsive canoe that he has used for well over twenty years now. I once poled down Green Brook with it, and discovered how easily it handled.

Often canoeing the Bartibog River, down from above the Bathurst highway in the summer, he would see along the banks places were deer came down, and birch stands where partridge fanned themselves in the sun. Content with his fishing, he would make a note of this, and one clear, crisp fall Saturday, he took his rod to fish some late salmon and decided, since it was deer season, to bring his shotgun. (The old-timers did this often in the early part of the last century, and "sports" would come up from the States for just such an event.)

He put in about a mile above the mouth of Green Brook, a fertile trout brook that runs into the Bartibog about three quarters of a mile or so above the Bathurst highway. That day, poling down the pastoral river with its small rushing rapids here and there, its water brownish green, stopping now and again to fish, he was able to shoot a few partridge that he saw fanning themselves along those side banks. Then, just at dusk, when the river sounded like all the musical instruments in the world, and the day was fast ebbing away, with the tall spruce shading the river and the leaves of maple and birch trees tinged gold and red, he saw a large buck come down to the water and start to cross to the far side. He was able to down it from seventy-five yards, as the canoe glided silently along. That night he poled down the Bartibog with a buck deer and salmon in the canoe. This must have made his father, a hard-fighting veteran of the Second World War, a fisheries officer, and a fine woodsman, very proud.

He began to do this each season at least once. The canoe was silent on the water, and being able to look from the river into the woods gave him an advantage that he felt walking or standing did not. The days, too, were a treasure, just before the river made ice, and the sun still warmed the earth by noon. He found it immensely pleasurable, whether he lucked in or not. It was, in fact, something of a fabled hunt, the autumn water filled with fish and clear and cold, the canoe gliding down with the slightest pressure from his pole.

One time he brought a friend to sit in the bow, rifle across his belly, who seeing a deer crossing the river far below them, fired at it three times, missing it each time. Finally David put his pole down, letting the canoe drift with the current. He grabbed the rifle from the fellow and fired just as the deer was coming out of the water. The deer dropped with one shot. It was a 190-pound buck. Other times he would pole for a while and, seeing some deer sign, he would leave the canoe and walk up into the small groves beyond the water and hunt the deer from that position, deep back in the Bartibog, a place very few hunters ever see. He took a large buck one day, leaving his canoe for a romp through a ridge of hardwood, and often as not he was successful.

He was and has been content with his hunting for many years now. But cynicism has also crept into his world. He is not fond of how many bucks are taken now, since the doe season is closed. He is also aware of how many does have been shot by accident, by hunters too quick to fire before they make sure, and left in the woods. For no one wants to bring out a doe without a doe licence. This is a terrible and hidden tragedy of hunting. While taking only males puts pressure on the buck, on the genetic blueprint of the herd, people must be aware that holding big buck contests in every nook and cranny of the province also leaves small bucks shot and abandoned in the woods as well. To say this might sound cynical, but hunting can be a cynical business. I myself have known men who were sure, raising the rifle to look through the scope, that they saw horns, and fired, only to walk up to a small doe, mortally wounded. Panic sets in. They know that they could be charged and lose their rifles and their vehicles, and so they abandon the doe to the coyotes. This does not help anyone, least of all the animals. But the big buck contest is fraught with the same kind of sentiment, so some (*some*) might leave a four-pointer in the woods because they are sure they will get a twelve-point later on in the season, so that they might enter a contest to win a four-wheeler. All of this is just greed and stupidity.

But David also has, as he told me one night, hunted enough. He has been on bad hunts, but not many. There was one time he mortally wounded a moose and couldn't find it, though he searched all one long night and all the next day. By the time he found it, the meat had been tainted. He still remembers that with agitation and sorrow. But the deer hunt is, to him, the best hunt, the most rewarding and the most challenging. The days can freeze you solid, and you are pitted against vast, uncompromising nature in an elemental way. This is the secret that real hunters have—that is, their desire for the rawness of the hunt overcomes all obstacles to it. In fact, the conditions are a prime motivator, for sunny, leisurely days are not conducive to it. Most hunters I know come alive in conditions that would make many stay inside. This is a fact of life. And they greet it by being alive. One of the biggest deer I shot was taken in a raging blizzard years ago. I decided that I would hunt the area I had prepared to hunt, no matter if it was storming or not. With the heater almost nonexistent in my old Suzuki jeep, I travelled up the twenty-five miles only to walk another two into the woods. There, almost freezing, and finding it hard to hold the rifle, I started out, only to meet the buck moving up the woods road toward me, the very storm drifting off his back.

One time my father shot a buck—this must have been back in the 1950s, or early '60s. He tracked the deer down across the roadway, and found a lot of blood in a ditch, was sure the deer had travelled no farther than that. Later, sometime in late fall or early winter, getting his hair cut, he was told a story by a man who declared that up on the Chaplin Road, earlier in the year, a buck deer had sauntered out of the woods and dropped in front of his car.

I suppose people are people and will do what they do. It is not reasonable to assume honesty in a hunt any more than anyplace else. But for some reason you do expect this.

You do not expect a man to come back to camp and tell you he has shot a huge doe by accident, and is frightened, so he has simply left it there. But this happens. It is not too hard to see horns that aren't there when you are excited. I suppose you can be talked into seeing them, at any given time. The way the deer blends in with its surroundings sometimes allows you to think that the branches above its head are tines. This is not such a far-fetched thing.

One year a friend of mine was hunting in a blind and watched a buck approach, on the last day of the season. He waited for a shot, and finally raised his rifle, saw the buck's antlers, and waited for it to raise its head. It took only a minute or two for him to realize his mistake—the buck had kept moving, just at an angle away from his scope view, and he had his rifle trained on a branch that he swore looked like buck antlers. By the time he realized his mistake, the buck was beyond him, and turning his rifle, he wasn't able to get a shot away. It was a silly mistake, he knows, but it did happen.

A few years ago, up on the Miner's Road, just before the Miner's Bridge, in off a logging road and along a back trail, I trained my rifle on a deer, and waited—waited it seemed forever—for it to show its head. I could make out its body, and had a clear shot—but I couldn't tell by this, by the way it was standing, if it was a doe or a young buck.

I didn't fire, and I am glad of it, because when it finally turned and bounded away, it was a doe—a big one; but a doe nonetheless.

There was also the case of my friend Peter McGrath who one day hunting saw a buck cross the road up along the Sheephouse stretch and fired, only to see he had shot a doe with horns. An anomaly, to be sure, but there you go.

Peter McGrath and Les Druet own a camp up on the main Norwest, and have had great hunts in and about their area. It is a camp that looks out across a beaver pond, and a marshy inlet, and over the Norwest Miramichi in the distance as it flows below the Portage River. Peter's main hunt is moose, though he has taken many deer along the Sheephouse, and up along the Johnson Road. He, too, is a guide without being a guide—many people rely upon his or Les Druet's expertise to help them find game. I have seen him take large buck in a chop-down, and he is a hunter who refuses to stay in one place, which is the one infuriating aspect of being with him. He will simply decide at any given moment, no matter how much proof to the contrary (in fact he could be standing in a fresh buck track), that he is wasting his time where he is, and will decide, on the spur of the moment, to go in an entirely different direction, because, as he says, he can "sense something" or has a "bad feeling" or a "good feeling."

Once, on the Sheephouse Road, he took his three-wheeler from the back of his half-ton and travelled to the end of the road, and into the woods another mile, and climbed to a tree stand he had made there earlier in the year—all in a blizzard. Once situated in the stand he came to his senses and realized that the blizzard was so bad he could hardly see the ground. So he got down, took his three-wheeler, and drove back to his half-ton, and made his way out to camp. All in a day's work, so to speak.

But he has had success nonetheless, and has shot a bull moose to the ground charging him at forty yards. He is one of the best hunters I know.

In fact, the last moose he shot he had called from the camp porch the first morning of the hunt. He called the long and mournful cow call, and, putting the horn down, he went inside for a cup of tea. Looking out the window he saw in the far-off distance something crossing the river (initially he thought it might be a bear). Taking a closer gander at it, he realized it was a bull moose that had responded to his call. He went out and called again. The moose came out of the river and abruptly disappeared in along the marshy ground, among high old grass and alders. He took his rifle and went down, walking the narrow planks over the old beaver pond. The moose was nowhere to be seen, so, standing in a small opening in the field, Peter decided to entice the animal again by giving the bull call. He gave the short, deep grunt of the bull.

"*Uugguh,*" he called. (This is a challenge to any bull in the area.) And again "*Uugguh.*" And as soon as he put the old horn down, he heard a crash on his right and the bull, a large fourteen-point, eight-hundred-pound animal, came running toward him. He raised his rifle and fired, and the bull dropped about forty yards away. The bull got up again, and came again, and it was the second shot that was the killing shot.

"I've had some close calls," he said, "but that may have been about the closest—doncha think?"

13

There are anomalies of another sort. How can I say this without being laughed at? Well, I can't, and I can't verify it, either. But being brought up close to the woods, to its vast hold over my mother's people, for instance, I have come to think that there are more things in heaven and earth than are dreamed of in my philosophy, to quote the Bard.

That is, perhaps there are ghosts in the woods, and they allow themselves to be known only when woodsmen are alone.

My Uncle Dow died when he was a child six years of age, falling on a jackknife. This is a story from the 1920s that fits into any time in the 1940s or '50s, when people alone far up the Mullin Stream, or on the Fraser-Burchill Road, said they saw things no one believed. (Or they didn't tell them for years because no one would have believed them.) Hudson, my grandfather, left the lumberyard on hearing his son was ill. As he was walking, he looked to the far side of the river, where a road (much like the road to his house) suddenly appeared to run down through the gloomy old-growth trees, and on this road he saw a horse-drawn hearse, with large plumes on the horses' heads. The horses rushed right toward him, and then vanished.

He knew at that moment that this must be a vision of his child's death.

It is eighty or so years after Dow's death that a nephew he never knew, a man in his fifties slowing down with arthritis in both arms and hands, is writing about his death, which seemed to be told to his father by a phantom hearse. How ridiculous!

There are other stories I have heard.

One man saw a Native woman doing her washing and braiding her hair. When he got closer, the woman turned, smiled, and disappeared.

In another story, an old Indian man points in the direction of the falls, on Mullin Stream, late in the afternoon. A friend of mine swears to this day that the old man was there, yet when he went to speak to him, he disappeared into the evening air.

It fits into the 1960s, when the deer came out of nowhere and ran toward me, a boy who was hunting partridge that cold night.

A woodsman once told me that he had spent a day in the woods talking to an old fellow, dressed from the early 1900s, who told him he had hunted woodland caribou on the barrens in toward Big Bald Mountain, and that his "sport" was lost, and they must come and help. The woodsman ran to get his coat and, coming back out into the yard, could no longer see the old-timer. He said he thought the old lad confused, until a few years later he saw a picture in a lumberman's book, taken circa 1905, with a group of hunters from long, long ago. In this picture one of the men was the one who had come to his camp to tell him his "sport" was lost, in 1974.

This, too, is a silly story—except when the fellow told it, it wasn't silly. For to him, it had happened as surely as I am writing it.

These stories come from somewhere, from our own psyche, perhaps. Yet how many men mock these stories when safe in their own houses, and feel them when they are in the wood? That is, men perfectly able to call all or any of this ridiculous when on a road will begin to question everything ninety yards from that road, in the deep bush. I have not really met anyone yet who is frightened to stay alone in the woods, who has any particular fear—such as fear of coyotes, or bear, or bull moose in rut. Those things are hardly considered. But the agitation comes from some other quality, not only in our own psyche but in the very nature of all that the woods implies. This is, in fact, a part of the hunt as much as anything else.

"If you are up in Christmas Mountain and see the devastation that the wind wrought in 1995—and you are alone up there—well, I will just say if you believe in anything at all you will begin to pray," says a logging trucker I know. He is as self-reliant as most men, and said this without apology at all.

An older man, a friend of David Savage's, a grand old man of the hunt, tells the story about years ago hunting up in the raw fields of the Bartibog River and, coming on to dusk in a blinding snowstorm, seeing a huge deer with rocking chair horns—that is, a deer with horns more like an elk or caribou—standing in the field. This old gentleman has taken enough deer and moose in the woods to fill two chronicles, and he says he was not fooled here. He had five shots in his rifle (I am not sure what kind of rifle it was, but he had hunted with it for years). He took his first two shots standing, while the deer was broadside to him. Then he kneeled and took another. For his last two shots he lay on the ground and fired. The deer finally moved off without a sound into the trees. He thought this strange and didn't mention it for quite a while. But then the next year a young man dropped in to visit him, and told him the strange story of coming down the Bartibog to hunt and seeing, in a field far away along the Gum Road, this huge deer with rocking chair horns. It was standing broadside in the late afternoon, the sun shining off its back. He fired six shots at it, and it never moved. After the last shot, the deer turned and walked into the woods.

This deer with the rocking chair horns was seen again, farther up the Russellville Road later that year, and again fired at, again missed.

Then, a year later, one dark night, someone knocked on David Savage's door and told David he had shot this deer with the rocking chair horns that afternoon, and it was an ordinary deer. But David never got to see it, or the horns, and remains skeptical that this deer was ever taken. He believes it will appear again someday to some unsuspecting hunter in the depths of the Bartibog wilderness.

14

I began to learn about deer slowly, but when I did the world of the hunt was opened up for me. It is not a mysterious thing; it could be said that buck deer are predictable, just like all other things in nature. There is a season and a time for them, just as for birth and decay. The mating cycle might go on three or four good weeks, during the colder weather in November. The buck marks out his territory, telling other bucks and doe a bit about who he is. This also provides information to the hunter. The buck will come back around to check these marks at given intervals to see if the doe have called. They will do this in enclosed ground, like black spruce or fir, so that they might walk right up to you. (One deer I shot was no more than fifteen feet away when I first noticed him, and he noticed me.) But they will do this in wide-open spaces, too, like hardwood ridges, or in querulous territory, along ragged chop-downs, where man's machines have pulled roots and all from the ground and left nothing embedded except the remnants of a forest.

On a large chop-down once, waiting on a buck I knew was making its rounds there, I had no idea another hunter was waiting on another buck some three hundred yards up the chop from me. He did not know I was there, either, so blended we were. I have long worn deer musk during the hunt (I actually think it works, so more fool I), so even though he now and again smoked a cigar there was no way I could have smelled it, even if he had been close enough. Then, as darkness began to encroach upon me, and with no sign through my scope in any direction of any deer, I stood to leave. Just as I did, the fellow sat up and trained his rifle on me. I turned and realized I was in the crosshairs of a .308 semi-automatic, up on Urquhart Road, and that this might be the last breath I ever took. It happened that fast—and there was nothing I could do, for I was afraid to wave lest he fire. Except the fellow stood to get a better look, and lowered his rifle in a kind of apology. But as I left the chop, in the dark, shouldering my rifle, I dropped it. I picked it up, examined it, and believed it to be no worse for wear, which was a silly mistake on my part.

The next day I went back to that chop-down. This might have been twenty years ago now, and I doubt it is there any more—I believe the forest has once again claimed it. It was a cooler day and I was alone, except for the jays that now and again bobbed about near me looking for bread. I had my scope and field glasses, and I began to survey the corners of the chop at early morning, and periodically throughout the day. The one thing the day can be up in this quiet is monotonous, and it is patience that counts there. It was sometime after four o'clock in the afternoon when all of a sudden (and it certainly seemed like all of a sudden) I noticed something far across the chop that hadn't been there a minute before. I leaned slowly ahead, and raised my rifle, and looked through the scope—it was a buck, about ten points, standing face on two hundred yards or so away.

There were two things I should have done. The first is, I should have sighted in my scope that morning after having knocked my rifle the night before. That was just common sense, but I was too impatient to take the time. The second thing I did wrong was to lack patience in the shot. I could have waited until the deer turned sideways. But the last thing I have ever been accused of is logic. So I trained my sights on the small portion of the deer I could see and squeezed the trigger. I missed it. I leaned forward more, brought another bullet forward, and fired again. I came very close, but missed again. The deer turned and fled, without my being able to get another shot. I had been very foolish. I am certain I would have taken that buck if I had waited until it turned broadside. But then I remembered having dropped the rifle.

The next day I went out to the gravel pit near my mother-in-law's home and checked. That knock had jarred the scope, so it was firing very high to the right. I sighted the rifle in, and prepared for the next year's hunt.

Peter McGrath, just driving along in his truck, can spot game in a chop-down a quarter of a mile away. It is a location that he has been very successful in, and he likes the chop-down (as do many others) because it gives him both a place to blend in with the torn-up ground and a fairly open shot when the game comes. In fact, a chop-down is a very inviting place for a deer or moose hunter, and some hunters I know spend their entire hunt in one chop-down or another and do not go beyond them into the woods proper. In a way—as strange as it might seem—it is a romantic place to hunt, with its deer avenues between huge mounds of thrashed and torn earth. On the cold days, after a snow, tracks are everywhere.

Another place Peter and other people I know like to hunt is along power lines stretched out for miles through spruce and bog. Deer will cross these places steadily, and many hunters wait on the top of a power line ridge to watch across this opened space (sometimes about a hundred yards wide and miles long) for those deer. Sometimes, however, they see deer too far away for a practical shot, and many times they are interrupted in their hunt by someone else staking out the power line and aiming back toward them. Then it is best to move.

The power line is undulated, with valleys and hills, overgrown by small maples or poplar, and distance can be deceiving. You might think a deer is closer or farther from you, depending on where you are situated. Peter McGrath, hunting one day along the line near his camp, with a bit of raw snow down, saw a doe and fawn cross far down the line and decided to get closer, because the buck would be handy. He quickly and quietly moved down along the line, and realized the deer were about two hundred yards farther away than he had initially thought. Still, he walked until he could see the doe and fawn tracks in that raw November snow, and he moved into the woods to wait for the buck. Facing the woods along the deer trail he sensed something behind him and, turning, saw the buck walking toward him, coming from the same side at which the doe and fawn had entered. Peter believes another hunter had spooked this buck to unwittingly come toward him.

Still, chop-downs or power lines are not the hunt I prefer. To get into the woods far enough and wait on a rut mark is the way I am best able to "control" the hunt (if anyone can do that). I have no qualms about saying that I would be a poor tracker overall, but I am not a poor waiter. I can wait on deer for hours without moving a muscle—I have done this along the Fundy coast and the south branch of the Sovogle, and along the Norwest. If you are in the proper spot, the deer will come right out in front of you sooner or later. I do not use deer calls or bring deer horns with me to rattle. For some reason I always believed that these things weren't that effective, and that one should wait upon the deer in its natural environment naturally. If you believe something is not going to be effective, I will guarantee you, most likely it will prove ineffective. That is, belief in the divining rod brings the water.

But I have been with lots of others who use deer calls and rattles and they seem to work just fine. David used a call up on the Sovogle with me one year and had a buck coming to it. The buck moved away before we got a look at it, but it was no more then twenty-five yards or so away, in the thick alders.

His antler rattle has brought deer to him as well. Not only buck but doe will respond to a rattle of horns— imitating two bucks in rut fighting, or a buck scraping horns to mark territory.

To use a call or rattle during the bow season is probably effective, for most killing shots are taken at about thirty to fifty yards, and you have to bring the deer to you. My cousin has hunted with a bow successfully for years. The bow season starts earlier in the fall—leaves are still very much on the trees, and it is a close hunt. Much like Wayne Curtis hunting partridge with a slingshot and smooth stone, a bow hunter must get close to his quarry in order to take the shot. To start the arrow back on a 120-pound pull might be difficult, and requires a strong arm, but once the pulley action takes over, it becomes more diplomatic, and one can hold it on his quarry a much longer time, and spring it forward with tremendous force.

Of course, stands are now the thing, and people are mostly in trees, with their bows, waiting on the deer to travel beneath them. The killing shot with a bow is usually below the fore shoulder, between the upper rib cage and the heart. The deer runs after the arrow strikes, and weakness and loss of blood force it to lie down. The bow hunter usually does not follow it immediately but waits for fifteen or twenty minutes or more for it to weaken. It is easier to find then, and stillness is more beneficial to the meat. One man shooting a deer with an arrow, following it quickly, was on a desperate chase through the Black River area for acres, and lost sight of it a dozen times. If he had waited, the problems he faced may not have arisen.

Usually, though, deer taken by bow tend overall to be smaller animals. I am not saying large deer can't be taken by bow; I am saying it is essentially the time of year that just might allow the smaller buck deer to wander more than the larger, dominant, and rutting buck.

15

But sometimes—and I realize this as well—hunters are simply . . . simple.

A man I know fired through his truck window, while sitting in it, so excited he was at seeing a deer. I know a man who began to shake so badly when he saw a big buck up near our camp at Mullin Stream that he could not for the life of him raise his rifle. Nor did he know why.

One day, a man I know got out of the car and, taking his .22 semi-automatic, fired eight shots at a partridge on a limb twenty feet above him, and missed it every time (I'll swear to this on any Bible). The bird, in the end, seemed to be making fun of him, shrugging this way and that, bobbing his head, fluffing up his feathers, picking up first his right foot, and then his left. All of this in view of three men, who were by this time rolling on the ground laughing. Finally, the man, who had regaled us the night before with his hunting prowess and the hunting prowess of his tribe, got into the car, shrugged, and said in his soft, Micmac way:

"Well, you see—I decided to let it live."

Then he could not stop laughing himself.

There is a picture in an old book of a wispy boy with a huge nineteenth-century musket waiting for a bear who is approaching behind him. This is more or less what happened to a man I know, whom I went to the Norwest to visit. I saw him poking his head out of a blind, looking desperately into the chop for a deer, while a huge—and I mean *huge*—buck was standing behind him twenty yards away on the road. It took off when I came toward it.

Like the buck my father had to stop on the road for, in upper Blackville one afternoon in 1965. It wouldn't move, while men were hunting on both sides of the road, in the woods, and in the fields.

My father waited a moment then said to my brother, "Check the trunk and see if I brought my rifle."

My brother was able to get out and open the trunk and look before the deer decided to take off. (No, my father had not brought his rifle.)

Or the man I know who was high in a metal tree stand looking at the fawns beneath him, saying, "Little fawns, so tiny so far below," and turned to see if the buck was behind them, when something let go on the stand, and down it went, thirty-five feet in half a second, and came to a stop a foot before the ground. The man was still in his chair, his gun still resting across his lap, a fresh chew of tobacco in his mouth, and he was staring at the little fawns' legs, while the little fawns looked down at him.

Or the man who waited an hour, seeing a black bear down the road, for this bear to get closer so he could take a shot, and suddenly out of the woods, after all his waiting, came a backhoe to finish digging the hole that was started that morning, making the clump of dirt the man thought was the bear that much bigger, but not a lot closer.

Or the man who with his friend snuck up on, as he described it, "an entire herd or two of ducks." He'd poked his sixteen-gauge out, took the shot, and realized all of a sudden that they were his neighbour's decoys, and tried his best to slink away. When his neighbour told him the story that night, he feigned a kind of universal outrage: "Some kinda nuts like that there are still walkin' about in the woods—makes ya scared to do anything!"

Or the man hunting with a friend, tracking the buck backwards. Or the fellow with another friend, who was creating so much of a commotion my friend went to see if he was in distress, and saw him walking back and forth, his rifle shouldered as if he was in a military square, shouting orders at the top of his lungs at himself. Or the young man who went hunting with Mike Kenny one long-ago day, shot the first two partridge out of the tree, both head shots. And then later in the day, when a quota of birds were walking in the woods before him—that is ten or fifteen birds— so close one walked over his feet, he missed each and every one, so finally Mr. Kenny took the .22 and shot a few.

However, these events are universally knitted into hunts, of people and places, and autumns of daring and laughter long, long ago. Most of them are integral to the nature of the time and place, and the hunt would be far less if there weren't enough of them.

The boys drinking a cup of tea who decided to change the teabag, "because it was a little stale," and realized, much to their surprise, that the teabag was a mouse.

16

I have said that those who eat meat should, at least once in their lifetime, kill that which they eat. I think this is a philosophical and moral duty. I think being a vegetarian is fine, but one should not be forced to practise vegetarianism. I am also saying that in my experience most hunters do no more killing than that. That is, the majority of hunters never kill many deer or moose. Some never kill any. Others only one or two. The idea that there is a great killing field is not evident upon examination—at least not with reference to the average hunter. The average hunter does not belong to the contemptuous class of killer who takes whatever he can. Those people are not hunters, and no law in the world would stop them. For those who act with such lack of restraint are bound by no law. The average hunter is shamed by them, and because of them shamed as well. You will not stop them by laws or decrees; they will only stop if forced from the woods (and this is unlikely), or if they come to realize that killing like this shows a lack of personal self-respect. That might sound silly, but I've known men who, once having realized this, have discontinued the practice that caused it.

When I was young there was a ban on moose hunting. It has been reported, and I have been told, that Louis B. Robichaud promised to end this ban, and therefore won the election in 1960 and became premier of our province. It shows the power of the tradition, the way of life we have tried to keep here. We have not succeeded completely, still, I do not know if we have failed.

My friend the Acadian sculptor Donald Dorion told me that he chiselled out of stone a giant moose, to be his offering to the god of the woods, for keeping him alive as a child. "For moose kept us alive for the first ten years of my life," he said. I have no reason not to believe him. My friend Hazel Francis Wood, a Micmac woman, says that moose didn't have the nutrients to keep her people alive, and she herself could not hunt anything, but she also recognizes in the same breath, and with a good degree of pride, that her brother is an excellent hunter. At the same table, another friend of ours says that moose is what she ate all during the harsh years of childhood, and she is thankful for it. My friend Giles Kenny, whose father, Mike, was one of the finest woodsmen I have had the privilege to know, says he himself has hunted enough and will not hunt again. He has killed and will not kill again. While at the same table on the same evening, another friend of ours says that not to hunt closes us off to a life that is both tradition and honour.

All views are discussed among the men and women I grew up with; each person has come to their own place in their heart in their own way. But what is essential to me is that no one at the table makes light of it. All of them know too much about it—and none of them make light of the animal that is hunted, which to me is perhaps the worst thing any hunter can do. Not to have respect for the animal is a blasphemy and I do not listen to it. If you do not respect the animal you hunt, then you do not have knowledge of it. You might end up snaring it in the woods, and allowing it to suffer unconditionally because of greed, and you would never honour it by chiselling it out of stone.

The idea of having an animal suffer is appalling to almost every hunter I know, and certainly every hunter I have come to respect. My youngest brother was with Giles Kenny's father, Mike, near his camp one cold autumn day. My brother walked right by something in the ground that Mike himself noticed. It was a tin barrel cut into wedges and buried in the ground to be used as a snare for moose. It would have been as much of a torture for the moose as some implements of the Spanish Inquisition were for hapless victims in the fifteenth and sixteenth centuries. My brother told me that he never saw a man so angry as when Mr. Kenny noticed this. He hauled it from the ground and kicked it to pieces.

When I was down south, I infrequently shot a coyote along the Fundy coast. I did not feel particularly terrible about this. I know they have a right to live—but when doing it, I thought of deer in the deer yards in winter, and their plight against the coyote.

At certain times throughout the winter, Peter and Les will bait coyotes near their camp on the Norwest. (Others will do this as well.) Even so, they are hard animals to corral and harder to shoot. Coyote are tenacious and smart.

Sometimes only the bait (horseflesh, usually) can be seen moving. They approach the bait almost on their bellies and from angles that often prevent a clear view. (One crawled on his belly behind me one November day along the Fundy coast some years back. At first I thought nothing much of it, but lately I have been of the opinion that he was thinking of jumping my back. And if I had not turned he might have.)

Coyotes can be found everywhere here now. And in cities, too.

Once I was walking on Hillsdale Avenue in the heart of residential Toronto and saw a scraggly dog approaching me. When afforded a better look, I realized it was a coyote. A few weeks later, playing golf with my son on the eighth tee at the Flemingdon Park Golf Club, in residential Toronto, a coyote walked (not ran) in front of us, across the seventh green and down into the ravine below. She was nursing, and her pups must have been somewhere down there.

Often on those bleak days along the Fundy coast, with the fog coming in off the bay, I would stand in an alder swale and watch a deer trail covered in an inch or two of snow, broken windfalls, and pulped leaves. Now and again a coyote would cross so low to the ground, the very colour of those leaves, that I would have to determine whether or not I actually saw something.

Something else happened when I hunted along the Fundy coast, in the southern part of our province, years ago. Deer were plentiful there, and the narrow trails to and from the secluded rocky beaches, surrounded by jagged cliffs, afforded the deer access to the salty shoreline, where they moved in the later part of the day. They bedded down at night in the high ground above the water, which had excellent cover for them, of alder swale and hardwood. Many days I would arrive just after sun-up, and take a position in the swales among the various pathways that led out to the beach. I would stay there during the day, hardly moving until dark. There the deer would pass unaware of my presence, small doe and fawn mostly.

So my brother and I saw many deer there, and each of us took a buck on the same day, ten years ago now—perhaps the last time I seriously hunted. My brother took his four-point buck with a bow, which is what he hunts with now. It was a killing shot at forty yards, and the buck was dead within five minutes of being hit.

When we were there we saw old graveyards—one from the 1850s and another from the 1880s. The people buried there were part of a failed community, a place that didn't make it—a people whose descendants moved on, and they were left to themselves in graves that were overgrown and forgotten under those turbulent Fundy skies. They were people from the 1850s, part of the Irish immigration to our land, part of my ancestry as much as any other.

Last year, when my brother was in the village registry office talking about land he once owned there, a person told him very excitedly that they had finally discovered the graves of those ancestors—that they had been hunting for them and hadn't known where they were exactly. It was a strange thing for us to learn—that just by accident we could have helped them discover what they were searching for much sooner.

17

What Disney did—as many writers, naturalists, and biologists tell us—was humanize animals, make their environment a utopia, and criminalize anyone who would enter what essentially is portrayed as Eden.

In Disney's Eden, the lions do lie down with the lambs. Deer play with wolves, and the trees and valleys are places of eternal bliss. Only when man enters is this bliss sadly disrupted. The idea that this bliss never was—that animals prey upon animals, that white-tailed deer take over moose habitat, and that all vie for life in a world of danger and death—is not conducive to the kind of propaganda that satisfies urban sentiment, and this is one of the falsehoods that anyone who lives near the woods understands.

That is not to say that those who recognize this error do not believe that the world of the woods is beautiful and aesthetic—it is, however, to say that things must be placed in perspective. Seeing *Bambi* as a child, and coming home to a father and uncles who hunted, was a clear disconnect with what the world wanted from me. For these movies and television plays want as much from their audience as they are ever prepared to give. What they demand is a kind of enlightenment about a world they have intentionally made false in order to achieve the result.

Besides, the woods are used in a multitude of ways by urban environments that are far more destructive to their inhabitants than hunting. This fact, if acknowledged at all, is simply written off as the price of urban living. But I will guarantee that many urbanites don't think of it at all as their problem. They believe it is a rural problem, and consider blaming those closest to the woods, charging them with implementing solutions. But in spite of this, clear-cutting is not done primarily for rurals, papermaking is not done primarily for rurals, lake and river pollution is rarely seen in rural Canada—and deer are more plentiful now than they were a century ago in hundreds of places in North America.

When I was Writer in Residence at the university in Fredericton some years ago, I was the only one in the department who went hunting. It seemed a long-established point of view that those who were educated, men and women, did not do this, and found it beneath them.

This was so prevalent a "feeling" that one of the professors, who was born thirty miles from my river, used to talk about how nervous he was to go there, because "our car might slam into a moose." He distanced himself from a place in his own province in order to coddle men who had never been there. This demeaning sleight of hand was considered, of course, progressive.

My Uncle Harry hunted for many years with just a twelve-gauge shotgun. I think it is a part of our blood, for this, somewhat like bow hunting, means a close hunt. One day, he told me, he stood on an old lumbering bridge that had not been used in years. It crossed a small rock-strewn stream somewhere on a side lumbering road up in the Norwest region of the Miramichi. His friends moved on, went to different parts of the area, but he decided to stay on the bridge. And he said:

"They moved off, and I was alone. It was a small, half-rotten bridge secluded in trees, and the woods had grown up about it again. I ended up standing there for hours watching the ripple in the water forty yards downstream, thinking to myself a deer had to come out sooner or later. It was just a feeling about how the little maples hung over the water and the space between them. It was just an instinct, a feeling I had. It was a pretty damn warm day, but I was confident, and never left my position. I know others would have given it just a look and kept going but I was sure, this is where deer were crossing. At about 4:35 in the afternoon, I saw something near the small maples that hadn't been there before. It looked like a brown part of a tree. I watched it intently for a minute or two, and suddenly it disappeared. I waited, and it appeared again, and stepped out exactly where I thought it might. I raised my shotgun and took it with one shot—a six-point buck."

That certain instinct, whatever it is and wherever it comes from, serves a good many hunters well. I know that Mike Kenny told me this the one day I hunted with him. He said to me, too, that sometimes you just "know" the deer is going to be there. I think when you hunt at close quarters this feeling can come over a hunter and benefit him greatly.

But the feeling comes at other times as well, when we are not at such close proximity. Peter McGrath and I were hunting one day up at Sheephouse, on the Norwest Miramichi, and had come back to the truck to have a cup of tea in the afternoon. It was strange, but at the exact same moment both of us looked down along the old lumber road and saw a deer crossing. Both of us saw it at the same moment, and both of us somehow knew we would. It was, however, too far away to get a good shot, and neither of us took a shot at it.

But at close quarters the feeling is more intense. One day down on the coast of New Brunswick, in among some swale, I stood, I swear, for five hours solid—remembering not only the story my uncle had told me, about the deer and the maple, but reminding myself that deer had to follow a certain ritual, and this would bring them out in my direction. Well, I was sure there were deer around me that day—I knew there were, but I didn't see any. I went home, slept, and got up early the next morning. As soon as I stepped into the woods, I swear I could smell deer. However, most people would tell me that what I smelled was simply the musk of rotting leaves and dying grasses at the end of the year, and the stale waters of fallen snows. Still, just as I had when I was a boy hunting partridge, I smelled deer, and I found a comfortable spot, and leaned back in some grass and waited. I waited for one hour, two, three hours, four. I never moved except for breathing. Suddenly it simply came over me. There was a deer coming toward me. I couldn't see him, but I sensed there had to be. I stood with my rifle at my shoulder, and was staring at a buck no more than twenty-five yards away.

I told this story about, and some people believed and agreed with me, and others said it was just luck, and I was not a good hunter, just a lucky one. Well, it was luck, but I knew I would have luck that day. A strange occurrence.

There is also the story that David Savage told me about being in close quarters when he shot the huge non-typical eighteen-point buck down in the Saint George area of the province. It was pouring rain, and early on they had seen some doe. But he and his friend were in among some alders and dead grasses and old-growth trees, and they could see very little. His scope, too, was continually fogging. That is the problem with scopes, especially in poor weather, and he was being rained on for over three hours. He said he finally told Jim Martin, his friend, that he was going back to the camp to get dry. He stood, and saw the eighteen-point non-typical, staring back at him about fifteen yards away. So he, who is one of the finest hunters I know, did not sense it. But I am sure in his life that he has sensed much else while hunting.

It brings me back to the rather ludicrous point that hunters sometimes "know" beforehand that they are going to see game. In fact, I'm willing to say that this sixth sense, on a few occasions, predicts the future. Oh, I know I will be heckled by those who are stingily correct about everything and right about nothing. But there is this fleeting nanosecond moment that has come upon me, and others, when we know we will see a deer an instant before we do. What or who tells us this? What or who directs us to look up at that moment? I do not know. But it has happened. Once, in a lonely field far off the main highway going to Heath Steele Mines, I suddenly turned and knew I was going to see a deer if I started to walk back. That was long ago—one of my first hunts—and I did see a deer but never got a shot.

It happened to my brother-in-law the first time he saw a deer in at the Mullin Stream camp. He told me, and I believe him, that he knew he was going to see it a second before it came out on the road. It was like predicting the future. But seeing it caused him to be too excited to take the shot—a case of "buck fever" that he has long since overcome.

I watched a program once in which people were involved in an experiment predicting the future. Now this was a very technical experiment. What they were asked to do was stare into an optometrist's viewfinder in order to watch flashing lights that were directed first toward one eye, then the other, in a random pattern, so one never knew at which eye the flash would be directed. Yet at a certain point the subject was able to close the eye that was being targeted before the flash occurred, in essence predicting the future. A very humble predicting of the future, to be sure—but still, an example of the mind's unknown abilities. Did our ancestors forty thousand years ago have this ability? Quite possibly, and maybe even to a greater extent.

I think it was a hunt about twenty years ago. I was still in Fredericton, and had just finished a novel, called *Nights Below Station Street*. What I remember about this book is that I wrote a section about hunting in it, as I did in its sequels, *Evening Snow Will Bring Such Peace* and *For Those Who Hunt the Wounded Down*.

In the days when these three books were written I was at my most dedicated as a hunter. I knew if I put my time in I would get deer. I was comfortable hunting alone, and I knew the woods well enough. I hunted with others as well. I suppose it was the same as some people getting together for a curling bonspiel once a year or so. I went hunting—a few days with Peter McGrath, a few days with David Savage, and a few days with my brother. With Peter I would hunt along the Norwest Miramichi, with David I would hunt the Sovogle area of the Miramichi, and with my brother I would hunt the southern part of the province along the Fundy coast. These were good times hunting— and usually on one of these hunts I would luck in, or one of my hunting friends would. To tell the truth, I was just as happy if they, not I, lucked in.

In fact I remember people at a camp getting very angry when a deer that had been there all summer was shot by someone from outside the area. No one at that camp would have hunted that deer.

Of all the places I hunted, I believe the Fundy coast was the best. The hunting ground ran for miles above the rugged coast of the Bay of Fundy, where my brother owned 140 acres of land. Deer were plentiful there, and coves and small hidden back fields offered seclusion for the game. My brother's land ran to the bay through alder swales and hardwood and, in the middle, a grove of crabapple trees with small apples that became very sweet in the fall. There were both bear and deer there, and one had to be careful when coming upon those trees, which were surrounded by dense alder bushes, not to accidentally interrupt a feeding bear. I found the deer didn't run as heavy as the deer on the

Miramichi, but they were more plentiful. Perhaps the big buck on average weighed twenty pounds less, but I am only talking from personal experience and I could be wrong. Still, thinking of the great eighteen-point non-typical that David Savage took in the south of the province and comparing it to deer that Peter, Les, and others took in the north, the deer did seem somewhat smaller.

I went hunting there with my brother that year, long ago now. But I myself did not have my rifle with me. My brother had seen a lot of partridge down on his land, and one crisp November morning we decided that we would gather enough for a good stew, which we had not had in a while. So off we went in my truck, and with his twenty-gauge shotgun we managed to shoot five or six partridge along the side road that led from his property out to the bay.

I know I wasn't dressed warmly enough for this excursion, but I am not sure if that was the reason. At any event, in the next few days I came down with a cold and flu that kept me down for the next week and a half. That meant I didn't get out hunting with either David Savage, whom I had planned to hunt with, or my older brother, whom I had planned to meet up with at our camp on Mullin Stream. Perhaps it was fortuitous, perhaps not, but I missed, because of my illness, the storm that trapped hundreds of hunters in the woods—many of whom had had no idea the storm was about to descend, and just as many who had known but were unprepared for it.

David had wanted to come to our camp, and had planned his holidays around it. Like many avid hunters, he set aside at least a week of holidays for hunting. But when he phoned me, the night before I was supposed to drive up and meet him, I could hardly lift my head off the pillow.

"I can't go," I said. And to prove I wasn't shirking, I sneezed a lot. "But," I said, "you can go to my camp anyway. My brother might be in there tomorrow night, but he'll be happy to see you."

David said he would see, but I knew he wouldn't want to go to a camp where he didn't know anyone. And I felt bad, and apologized for letting him down. But there was little or nothing I could do about it.

That night he made his way up to the Mullin Stream area alone, past the bridge across the Narrows—one of the finest places on the entire south branch of the Sovogle. The area, though worked and clear-cut at places, is still a rugged and pristine land, filled with streams and heavy woods. It gets cold and snowy on the high ground earlier than in the valley, and one can feel the bitter air by mid-October. David travelled another sixteen miles from the bridge across Mullin Stream, at the Narrows. There he met a man he knew, who had his huge trailer parked at 2.2 Mile Road. That, to him, was the best of luck, for that was where he wanted to hunt anyway—it was an area, about five miles or so from our camp, that ran above the South Branch, proper, where David had taken two or three deer in the last few years, and he was a firm believer that he could luck in there.

"So I was set," he told me. "Blair was there with his trailer—and although he hadn't lucked in as yet, I was certain we would see something the next day. I was still thinking I might go into your camp for an afternoon if I had time, but I thought I would get a deer here. In fact, I was sure I would. There was some snow down, and I was hoping to get on some tracks in the morning. It was still light when I got there, and I took a short walk into the woods, toward the river. There I picked up a trail of a doe and fawn—and saw a buck track, too, but not a large buck. I came back into the trailer and cooked up some deer steak that night. We had a game of cards and got to sleep."

At the same time, my brother had gone into our camp, and if he was still waiting for me or not I didn't know. I had told people I would be in but, of course, circumstances were such that I couldn't make it. He was there with a friend, Ken Francis, and they too had scouted the area where my younger brother John had taken the eight-point a few years before. They had seen many tracks, and were actually hoping for a new snowfall to help them along—I think perhaps everyone was, at that moment. In camps all over the Norwest, men were preparing for the hunt: oiling their rifles, checking their sights and scopes, making last-moment decisions about what direction they would take. It cost a few their lives.

At that moment, across the province, somewhere north of the town of Plaster Rock, my friend Peter McGrath was staying at a camp with some people he had worked a motor plant shutdown with that summer. He was invited to the place, and if the people are convivial, and there is a place to hunt or fish, Peter will be there. I have often telephoned him only to find that he has been bass fishing here, or salmon fishing there, or duck hunting somewhere else, with a variety of people whose names I had not heard before. "I met a lad at work," he would begin, and regale me with a story about a hunting or fishing trip that three days before he'd had no idea he would be on. In fact one year, a few weeks after he got to Toronto, where he was working a shutdown at Ford, he told me where deer were, and partridge, for he had been out scouting the land on the perimeter of the largest city in Canada. I am sure that this is how he was, is, and will be until the Lord takes him home. Now he was in a large hardwood ridge filled with brooks and streams that ran for miles down into the Saint John River, and he was preparing to hunt a section of wood he didn't know.

The snow started early the next morning before light— before any of the hunters had woken—but by the time my brother and Ken were up, the day was already heavy with snow. After their breakfast of bread and tea, my brother took his twenty-gauge, and a couple of slugs, and started up the old road, toward the washed-out bridge, while Ken planned to hunt back behind the camp. By the time my brother got across the bridge, Mullin Stream had just made ice, the snow was about five inches deeper than the night before, and he soon picked up tracks that led up from the river into the old spruce and fir stands above the tractor road, which he decided to follow. He was sure the tracks belonged to a buck and doe, and he felt very confident he might luck in by noon hour.

The snow was at least as deep up in the Plaster Rock area, where Peter was, and he was out alone along the hardwood ridge, where the snow fell in large flakes all across the width and breadth of the giant birch stands. It made the day gloomy, and it was difficult to see far, and he was continually clearing his gun scope and trying to keep it clear. Here, Peter said, tracks were everywhere, and "as soon as I was on one I would see another more promising." One year, sitting up on a hardwood ridge, Peter was scanning the side hills and distant spaces between the large trees for the sign of deer, when, looking straight out, he suddenly realized there was a buck standing fifteen feet away, staring straight at him. Though he was not as fortunate this day, and in no way was the visibility as pure, he did see many signs, he saw a few doe, and he was sure if he kept on his toes he would have a shot at a buck. The thing was, it kept snowing, and he kept travelling.

He had come a long way from the day he had, on the Miramichi side of Plaster Rock Highway, gotten so turned about on the rugged hardwood ridges that he was sure he was lost. For one thing, he now made sure he carried a compass when he went into unknown territory—especially along ridges. But he knew as well that this snow was unusual, and that it looked as if a major storm was brewing. He continued, however, to move away from the camp he was staying at, move farther into the myriad of hardwood, where the deer were moving freely in rut as the snow got deeper. By noon it looked as if it were three o'clock, and the clouds were low.

David Savage was up at dawn and that morning hunted the right side of the 2.2 Mile Road, that is, the side farther away from the river. He had passed up a doe (though he had his doe licence) and he was concentrating on a giant set of tracks, which he followed most of the morning. At about ten o'clock he sat down and opened his small rucksack for his lunch of tea and corned beef sandwiches. The snow now obliterated the buck's tracks, but trailed away across the 2.2, and he decided the deer must have been checking its scrapes back down toward the Sovogle River. So after his tea, he strapped his rifle on his shoulder and started out again, following the slurred impressions of the large buck, toward the river both of us, and Peter and Ken and Bill, had fished many times, on sunny days. He went down almost to the river, and waited until well into the afternoon.

By afternoon, as the snow fell over the trees and deepened in the hardwood ridge, Peter, some 150 miles to the northwest, found himself at least five and a half miles from the camp. The snow was now deeper than he had travelled in before, and deeper then he'd imagined it would be. He had, well, cigarettes and matches, a half pint of rum, and some candy bars. He had no change of clothes, no extra pair of underwear or sweater. And as the wind picked up and began to drift over the footprints he would use to travel back out, he wondered if he was not to be stranded there. It was difficult to see very far. On good days he would be able to see from one far-away ridge to another, and with his scope check movement at five or six hundred yards. But now he could see no more than five or six yards altogether, and it was worsening. His beard was frozen, and so too had his eyelashes turned to ice.

"I knew I had to find a shelter or get the hell out of where I was," he said. He had his fur-lined hood up, which mightn't be the smartest outerwear except for the fact that he seemed totally by himself in these ridges, and the snowfall was becoming harder and turning all the trails into almost identical topography: a blur in front of him, and a blur to the side, and a blur behind. He turned and made his way in the direction he thought he had come, checking the compass once. He headed out toward the southwest, uncertain which ridge he was on but at least certain, this time, that he was heading the way he wanted.

At some point in the afternoon David's friend shot that doe, hung it in the trees for the night, and made it back to the trailer. David, too, made his way back toward late afternoon, when the storm was so bad he felt he couldn't see anything in front of him, and it was useless trying to keep his scope clear. Every time he lifted it, it was filled with fog. So he started back, while a whirlwind surrounded him. He got to the trailer at about five that afternoon, told Blair about the big buck he was tracking, and, as he and Blair had supper, Blair told him about the doe he had taken. David spoke about getting the doe that was hung in the tree in the morning, but there was no way they could get it now. They sat up late, listening to the sound of the storm as it closed in upon them, wondering if they would be able to leave the 2.2 anytime soon.

My brother and Ken both had a long, hard day as well. My brother didn't want to give up on the deer he was tracking, but the tracks became blotted out by one o'clock that afternoon, and as he walked, thinking he was still in the spruce wood above the tractor road, he realized suddenly that he had crossed behind the end of that road, and was in the thicket near where my brother John had taken the deer a few years before. The only reason he knew this was because of a great old oak that stood alone, and rose up above the surrounding spruce, that he knew was well to the east of that tractor road. He had gotten there by crossing a road that was now completely snowbound. Realizing this, at about two that afternoon, he made his way back, toward where he thought the road would be, and finding it, as the day was fast becoming unlivable and dark, he made his way south toward the cabin. Ken also had come back from the woods, without seeing any game that day. For a while they waited, for me, thinking I would be coming in. I hadn't been able to tell them I was in bed sick and unable to get there. At seven Bill went out to the end of the 17 Mile Road, to see if I had gotten my jeep stuck, but finally came back, unconvinced I was safe but not knowing what else he could do.

It was late afternoon when Peter made it down to a brook, from which he believed he had left earlier that morning. But it was now past twilight, and he had over a mile and a half still to travel. The storm ferocious, he didn't know if he should attempt it. His beard frozen solid and his hands and feet numb, he saw a small cabin at a point in that brook where an old road came down. He decided, if he could get in without breaking in, and light a fire, he would stay the night. And this is what he managed. He lit a warm fire in the stove, took his boots off, and dried out his socks and boots, then sat with his feet on the oven door and drank his rum. Unfortunately it caused his friends some major panic, and they all went out searching for him, well after dark, and worried all night where he might be. But be that as it may, he did the right thing, and perhaps the only thing he could do. He would move when the storm blew itself out.

The storm was over by Monday morning, and David Savage got up at first light. Huge drifts of snow angled along the old 2.2 Mile Road, where I myself spent days of my youth travelling from one fishing spot on the old South Branch of the Sovogle to the other. It meant that the main road into the Mullin Stream area was drifted over as well, and dozens of hunters were now stranded.

Blair had to get the trailer ready to leave—they didn't know if they could get it out onto the main Mullin Stream Road or not. While Blair began to get things packed, David took his rifle and went down the 2.2 to bring Blair's deer out. He had walked about two or three hundred yards, the world about him completely white and the sun dazzling on the new fallen snow, when he saw a spot far down the road, at a turn, almost four hundred yards away. He stopped, raised his rifle, looked through the scope, and saw the big buck he had been tracking two nights before. He had his 30-30 with him, and a four-hundred-yard shot at a deer with a 30-30 is a long shot. But David decided to take it. He fired once, and the deer seemed to go sideways just slightly and leave the road. David walked through those drifts, and down to where the deer had crossed, and saw no blood. But he did see a small, very small tuft of deer hair in the middle of the road. To him this was unusual, and he decided that, blood or no blood, he had come very close, so he followed the tracks into the woods, and within forty yards, he saw a spot of fresh blood, and then more. He followed the tracks, as the snow got deeper and deeper, and found more blood. Then he saw where the deer had fallen. He continued on, and then stopped and, looking to his right, saw where the deer had finally lain down, burying itself up to its back. When he reached it, it was dead—a ten-point buck, 240 pounds.

He dressed the deer with his small knife and then, using some rope in his pack and making a litter out of spruce poles, he hauled the deer back up the road, where he went into the spot where Blair had hung his doe in the trees. Bringing it down, he put it on the litter with the buck and hauled both back to the trailer. There they tied the deer down on the top, and Blair started his truck, and with David following they made it out from the Mullin Stream before almost anyone else.

Peter made it back to the main camp and apologized to those who had searched the area for him the night before, but, as he said, he couldn't help wanting to stay alive, and keep warm while doing so. It was not his last trip into the ridges along the western side of our province, and the next year he took a buck from that very place. Perhaps the buck that he had tracked in the great storm of November.

All about the province hunters became stranded in that storm, and many did not get out for some days. It was one of the worst November storms in memory. Three men would have died of asphyxiation if friends of mine hadn't come across them, their exhaust pipe buried in the snow of the road and their windows rolled up.

One man, finding himself overcome by deep snow, built himself a lean-to and planned to wait the storm out. He then tried to make his way out, but by Monday morning things seemed hopeless to him and he felt he was utterly lost, without food, water, or warmth. He kneeled in the snow and took his life, not knowing that he was less than half a mile from his car, and that searchers were only twenty minutes or so from discovering him. In fact, they thought his shot was a signal to them.

That though he believed he was abandoned, and forsaken, it was not so.

18

I have hunted most of my life. And I have always been of two minds. I loved the hunt, but I never thrilled at the killing. Still, that was a part of it. And I knew an animal living in the wild, even if taken after only four years, was given a better life than cattle. I hunted most areas with the idea that I was getting out in nature with friends, and that was a good thing. In the last few years I have taken a hiatus. I don't get back to my former ground in the fall of the year so much now. My guns remain in the cabinet, and I have .303 and .32 Winchester bullets in cases I have not opened. I have not drawn a bow in eight years. And though I love my New Brunswick home, I am often away. The days of my fall sojourns into the wilderness have become more a trickle than a flood. And I am reminded in the winter, when the sun is bright on the snow, and there are at times hawks in the Ontario sky, of days when the hunt was in my blood as much as anything I have ever done.

The first time I took my son John, some years ago, he was five years of age, and I brought my shotgun to do some partridge hunting.

It was November, but the day was bright and warm, and leaves were still on the trees. John, dressed in hunter's orange from head to foot, looked like an advertisement for hunter safety, and we drove into a side road, along the coast, where I had taken a deer the year before. There we spent the afternoon, me with the old Coleman stove that once belonged to my father. I heated up hot chocolate and set up some targets in a field for John to shoot with a small .22. I helped him hold the rifle and fire, and though he didn't hit many targets it was a kind of baptism, in a place and age where rifles and guns of all sorts are now in question. (I know a famous writer of wilderness tales who is terrified of rifles and the very wilderness he writes about— which is perhaps how things even out in this life.) But the main aspect of all of this was safety—and as much as I would have liked to have seen a partridge, it was not as important for us as taking a few practice shots.

Last year, the day after we drove the Maliseet hunters out to the village, my son and I went back to those hills. There was a good deal of snow, and the sky was blue and cold. John is now twenty-one years old and taller than his old man, who used to carry him on his shoulder across half the world when his mom and I were young.

The deer were moving—and we went to the road I had wanted to the afternoon before. I have put a scope on my .32 Winchester and my son John uses it. We arrived at 8:49 in the morning, walked to the brook, and realized it had made ice. We stood there no more than twenty minutes, on the other side of the chop where we were the day before. I knew it was only a matter of time. And a little four-point buck came walking toward us. I did not raise my rifle, and I told John nothing—that is, it was up to him. The buck turned, jumped high across the frozen water, and John fired as it went up toward the road our truck was parked on.

I showed him how to dress it, we hauled it up the bank in midmorning, and we drank strong, dark tea I made on the old Coleman stove. We took a picture for posterity—a simple moment between father and son.

So I have done what I said I would do, and it is not important if I hunt again.

I do not think that those I have met in Australia or other places know what snow means to the Canadian psyche and how much a part of us it has become. That there is in our very being the North Land, Strong and Free, I am not so sure any more. But the pulse it gives us is still a wild one. It is also a hot-blooded one. I have been out in nights of 35-below and lived, and so have those I have spoken about in this text. I am still amazed and gladdened by what men of the north woods can do, how they are self-reliant like few people. I have known enough men to know that there is enough credit and discredit to go around. Those who blame the English or the French or the First Nations for the problem of game management, etc., will never know the truth— that all men are countries and nations unto themselves.

We meet a new nation each time we stare into someone's eyes.

This fall they took a large moose at Peter's and Les's camp. Once again their expertise lucked in. I don't know any of my other friends who got a moose licence this year. I am away from the hunt now, and it is almost as if I have abandoned it, or it has abandoned me. I still know enough about it all, however, to know I would be able to once again take deer or moose if I put my time in.

Last year was the first year in many that David Savage didn't get his deer. He tells me that he doesn't care that much now. There is still enough fire in his voice when he gets to speaking about it all, though, that I know he knows he will hunt again. But so many of my hunting friends are wary of the rules and the laws, and the scent of officialdom on everything, and the "bucks only" tag that good hunters feel is a damage to the woods in the end.

Guns are now registered, and a special permit is needed to buy bullets. Some who refuse on principle to do this— and there is a principle involved—find themselves unable to hunt when the weather changes up.

My friends are growing older as well. When David Savage (and I've seen him pole a canoe down the Norwest with a broken leg) goes out now in his canoe to take birds from the gravel along the shore, or to spot a buck crossing with the light of the lowering sun on its back, he can remember more hunts than he probably has left. It has been fun, but someday it will be over. And with almost every drift of the canoe, and every jab of the pole, he can remember other times, other hunts, and the voices of men and women who are no longer here. His father, who died recently, poled this river before him for forty years, and so did his uncles and the fathers of his friends. He remembers the little doe hiding in the swale and a buck coming behind her to butt her up with his antlers so she would move and be safe. And seeing this, he couldn't fire.

This is a fine memory and important, because it shows that the animals, though not like a Disney creation, are still, all in all, a creation of God, able to live and breathe and anticipate, and deserve our understanding and respect.

David asks me if I will hunt again, now that my son John has taken his first deer, and I always say sure, though my guns more often stay in the cabinet, like Wayne Curtis's. Peter McGrath, too, is getting older, fifty-four now. I remember him in his teens, and as a young man, hunting and fishing alone along the little Souwest, a place of wilderness, salmon, deer, and bear, where he would fish and hunt from dawn, and get out of the woods after dark.

I think sometimes he has grown old hunting, and I am sure he knows that someday others will take his place. His beard is now greying, and he is not as young as he once was—though still and all a capable man. He still works in an industry where men use their muscle and blood to live, and grow old fast.

But he might prove me a liar, Peter, for even on the hottest summer days, he will travel eighteen miles upriver on his old three-wheeler to find a pool, and he can still shoot moose on a dead charge at sixty feet. Which not many have the guts to do. But then again, many people of the Miramichi would do and have done the same.

I have been surrounded all my life by men who are, for the most part, common men, and who are, for the most part, generous and noble and have in their hearts a life force that is undeniably proud.

The greatest hunt, I think, is from the canoe. I ask David about this, and he says it is. He tells me that he doesn't mind tracking, and tracking in snow comes naturally to him and he is able to do it well. But still and all, the canoe is one of the best ways to hunt.

My brother Bill built me a new cedar canoe last year. This is great for me, to get a canoe built by my brother, after the old canoe that I had for twenty years was—well, let's just say "misplaced."

Bill and his Micmac friend Kenny Francis of Big Cove started building canoes a while ago. Ken's people, of course, are masters, and Ken has built canoes from birchbark. But now he too is building cedar.

I plan to hunt along those stretches of that river I have fished, just once—caring nothing but for the experience of doing it, whether I see anything or no. When the day is bright and cool, and shadows of the trees lean against the water, and now and again an osprey is in the sky. A deer might come down to the river as you pole. And if it doesn't, so what? Many of the old-timers did this—there are hundreds of pictures of men transporting game back from the kill in a canoe. But the age has moved on, and the idea of being that much a part of the world is somehow no longer in fashion.

The men I have hunted with, and known since I was a child, have grown older, just as I have. In some respects I would not be able to tell the difference between them and a picture of hunting guides from the last century. During October and November their eyes are as sharp and beards as coarse as those of many old caribou guides from camps set up in 1905. They have lived the same kind of life, and in many ways expected no more from it. Some, like my poet friend Eric Trethewey, have lived lives probably at times harder and at least every bit as dangerous. To read Trethewey's essay "On Drowning" is to experience a small but brilliant glimpse into this world.

All of them have lived lives as worthy as the lives of anyone I have ever met. Most of them know animals as well as anyone I have spoken to, and have as much respect for them. I would trust any man I have mentioned in this text to speak with as much wisdom about the woods as anyone in the world. I said in my fishing book that someday, in some way, the world will move on, and the river will no longer be ours. That I am sure is true. But I am glad to have been a part of this generation when it was ours.

From: *For Those Who Hunt the Wounded Down*

Bines had told his son this story. It was just before Willie went to bed. Bines was sitting, facing his son, with his huge hands folded near Willie's knees. Every now and then Bines would touch those knees with his hands, and draw them away delicately.

It was a story about a deer and how it outsmarted a hunter. It was a story of the woods, of gloom and darkness, of autumn ending and winter coming on.

"This happened a long time ago," Bines said. "There was an old deer, who had been in many battles in many ruts, and this was its ninth year. It had been cold all autumn, and the trees were naked and raw. Far off it could see smoke from the hunter's house, rising in the sky. It had lost its strength—this old buck—and kept only one doe, who had a small fawn. The afternoons were half-dark and winter was coming on hard—and the hunter kept coming—the hunters always keep coming."

Bines looked over at Ralphie and smiled, and Ralphie nodded.

"The big deer didn't have no friends. He usually travelled alone. But he saw all the other deer being killed, one by one. And though he gave them other bucks advice—gave them advice—they didn't follow it.

"So all the other deer was killed, one by one. But the hunter who tracked him—who tracked the old buck in the snow—was smart as any hunter. The buck knew this, and wanted to keep him away from the doe and her fawn if he could. He was an old deer and the doe was young. So the big buck decided to draw the hunter to himself—and each day the food was more and more scarce, and each day it was colder. And each day it led the hunter farther and farther from the cabin.

"The puddles were frozen and the trees were naked, and the sky moved all day long—"

Jerry touched the boy's knees lightly again and smiled.

"Every day the hunter would get closer—get closer to the doe. But the buck had a plan, which it had learned from living so long. It would always show itself to the hunter at daylight and lead him on a chase throughout the whole day. The hunter could never catch up to it. At the end of every day when the hunter came to the river the buck wouldn't be there. The buck always disappeared—and its tracks disappeared, as if it had flowed away."

"Where?" the boy asked.

"The hunter didn't know—didn't know. No one did. The hunter too was tired. He was, a tired man. Each day he got up earlier. And remember—each day he wanted deer meat for his family. So he was only doing what he had to. Had to do there. Each day he concentrated on the buck—each day he followed the tracks to the river. Each day he found nothing there.

"And each day his children were hungry, his wife was sick. And each day the hunter was weaker and colder. And each day the big old buck had allowed the little doe and its fawn to live another hour, another night."

Jerry looked about the room, and the boy smiled timidly.

"The buck was old and tired but so was the hunter. The hunter had a bad hand and had wrapped it in his leg stockings. His eyes were fine and could pick out a small bird in a thick bush. He scanned the river every evening. The river was a wild river and had just made ice—a wild river there, but the ice was thin.

"One day after a heavy snowfall the hunter found himself deep in the woods—the sky had cleared, the stars was coming out—the hunter had been following the buck for many hours. It was hours I guess he had followed the buck that day.

"There wasn't a sound when the hunter come to the river.

"The day was solid and still and he cursed to think he had lost it again. Lost that buck there again. Now the stumps were covered and everything was quiet. Afternoon was almost ended—and night was coming on—and that's when he saw the doe. She was making her way along the riverbank, and he could just make out her brown hide by a tree. She was coming right toward him. It was almost dark. She hadn't seen him, and she was leading her fawn toward him up an old deer trail. The fawn behind her.

"So the hunter felt he must use this chance, and he knelt and aimed and waited. Everything was still. He cocked his old rifle and was about to fire—about to shoot it, you know. But then of course everyone knows what happened."

Bines paused and lit a cigarette. He smiled and touched the boy lightly on the knee once more.

"What happened?" Ralphie asked.

Bines drew on the cigarette and looked about.

"Everyone knows what happened," Bines said. "It has been passed down from generation to generation to all the smart deer in the woods."

"What happened?" Willie asked.

"The hunter aimed his rifle, and suddenly the ground moved—the ground under him—and the buck come up, from its hiding place under the snow, right under the hunter's feet—under his feet—everyone knows that—and snorting and roaring ran onto the river. The doe turned and jumped away, and led her fawn to safety.

"And the hunter made a mistake, mistake there—hunters always do sooner or later—I mean make a mistake there. He was so angry he didn't think straight.

"'I got you now,' he yelled, and he ran onto the river too.

"Now, that river could hold the buck, and it could hold the hunter. But it could not hold both together. And the buck turned and stood, waiting for him to come further out. The old buck never moved. And if he was scared he never showed it.

"And when the hunter got close the buck smiled—and the ice broke, and both of them went together—down together into the wild rapids—clinging to each other as they were swept away. And this story was passed down. It's a passed-down story.

"Now the end is going to come—in one fashion or another," Bines said, softly and again he turned to Ralphie and smiled. "We all know, the end will come. You either face your hunters or run from them."

Acknowledgements

I would like to thank Peter McGrath and David Savage, two men of the N.B. woods, and thanks also to my son John Thomas Richards who hunted with me last, and Anne McDermid my agent. Thanks to my brothers John and Bill, wife Peg and son Anton. I would thank also Les Druet, Bob Drisdelle and Jason and Wayne Curtis, and all the great men over the years, and great women too, who knew the value of what they said and did.

Special thanks to my editors Tim Rostron and Catherine Marjoribanks.